C000261294

STAFFORDSHIRE
& THE BLACK COUNTRY
MURDER CASEBOOK

Other counties in this series include:
Cheshire
Cumbria
Essex
Lancashire
Leicestershire & Rutland
Shropshire
Sussex
North Wales
South Wales

STAFFORDSHIRE
& THE BLACK COUNTRY

MURDER
CASEBOOK

DAVID BELL

COUNTRYSIDE BOOKS

NEWBURY · BERKSHIRE

First published 1996
© David Bell 1996

All rights reserved. No reproduction
permitted without the prior permission
of the publisher:

COUNTRYSIDE BOOKS
3 Catherine Road
Newbury, Berkshire

ISBN 1 85306 432 7

Produced through MRM Associates Ltd., Reading
Typeset by Techniset Typesetters, Newton-le-Willows
Printed by J. W. Arrowsmith Ltd., Bristol

CONTENTS

for Jack Bell (1908–1996)

ACKNOWLEDGEMENTS

I would like to express my thanks for help and co-operation to the *Express & Star* (Wolverhampton), the *Burton Mail*, the *Uttoxeter Advertiser*, the *Tamworth Herald*, the *Leicester Mercury*, the Staffordshire Police Museum, and to the Magic Attic newspaper archive in Swadlincote. I am also grateful for individual help generously given by Ros Prince, John Godwin, Alan Walker, Alan Lewis, Rex Dinsdale, Mark Green, Frances Cartwright, Mrs Lowe, Vic Good, Fred Brashay, Gordon Wain, Joan Cooper, Mrs N Hill, Vince Cresswell, Graham Nutt, Shirley Palin, John Walker, Tim Cockin and Ken Fallows.

INTRODUCTION

The concept of a Staffordshire county police force was discussed at a meeting of the Court of Quarter Sessions held in Stafford in October 1842, when it was agreed that a Chief Constable should be appointed. The force was to have three divisions. One was the Mining District in the south, including the towns of Bilston, Willenhall, West Bromwich, Wednesbury, Smethwick and Handsworth. This area had been policed by the South Staffs Constabulary since 1840, but would now come under the newly formed county force. The second area was the Pottery District in the north, and included the towns of Burslem, Hanley, Stoke, Fenton and Longton. The third district, known as the Rural District, would cover the rest of the county. The new county force would not cover the four towns of Stafford, Newcastle-under-Lyme, Walsall and Tamworth, each of which already had its own established police force.

In December of the same year, John Hayes Hatton, a 47 year old professional policeman, was appointed as Chief Constable of the Staffordshire Constabulary, a post he held for 15 years. The constables he recruited were trained in the yard of Stafford prison, but 95 of them either resigned or were dismissed in the first two years, unable to take to the severe, military style of discipline. The men were frequently fined for such 'major' misdemeanours as smoking a pipe or talking to prostitutes while on duty.

Although some of the independent forces soon came under the umbrella of the county police – Tamworth borough in 1857 and Stafford borough in 1858 – the traffic was not all one way. Lichfield city had its own police force from 1856 to 1889. Hanley, an original member of the Staffordshire Constabulary, left in 1870 to form its own borough force, and other Pottery towns joined it in 1910 to form the county borough of Stoke-on-Trent police force. Wolverhampton, another original member of the Staffordshire Constabulary, left in 1848 and had

STAFFORDSHIRE CONSTABULARY

WANTED respectable SINGLE MEN : age, not to exceed 30 years; height, not less than 5 feet 8 inches without shoes ; to measure 37 inches round the chest, be able to read and write, generally intelligent, free from any bodily complaint, and of a strong constitution. Good rates of pay, with clothing, boots etc.

Forms of application may be had at the Chief Constable's Office, Stafford, by applying personally or in writing ; or from any Superintendent, Inspector or Sergeant in the County.

Chief Constable's Office, Stafford, July, 1902.

An advertisement for officers for the Staffordshire Constabulary. (Staffordshire Police Museum)

its own force until 1968. The strongly independent Newcastle-under-Lyme borough force resisted amalgamation with Staffordshire until 1947.

There were further major changes in 1968. In the south of the county, all the Black Country districts – West Bromwich, Smethwick, Wednesbury, Bilston, Brierly Hill, Willenhall – became part of the newly formed West Midlands police force, along with Walsall, which had always maintained its own force. In the north, the Stoke-on-Trent county borough force amalgamated with the Staffordshire county police. In 1974, two further areas – Aldridge and Brownhills – were lost to the West Midlands police force, and the remaining force became known by its straightforward present name: Staffordshire Police.

Most of the county's Chief Constables served for relatively short periods of between four and 22 years. This is not surprising, since many had long years of service before being appointed to the top office. Arthur Rees, for example, had been Chief Constable of Denbighshire before becoming Chief Constable of Staffordshire in 1964 and the last Chief Constable, Charles Kelly, was previously Staffordshire's Deputy

Chief Constable. One exception was Colonel Hon George Anson, son of the 3rd Earl of Lichfield. When he was appointed in 1888, he was only 31 years of age. As he held the position until he was 72, he is not only Staffordshire's youngest ever Chief Constable, but also the longest serving. His period of office stretched from 1888 until 1929, a 41 year tenure that encompassed the Jack the Ripper murders, the Boer War, the Russian Revolution, World War I, the women's suffrage struggle and the 1926 General Strike.

The county police force was strongly resistant to the idea of female

Colonel Hon George Anson, Chief Constable of Staffordshire from 1888 to 1929. (Staffordshire Police Museum)

Sergeant Lily Broadhead, appointed to the Stoke-on-Trent police force in 1921. (Staffordshire Police Museum)

police officers, and it was not until 1944 that six women constables and a sergeant were appointed. The Stoke-on-Trent police force was more progressive, however, appointing two women officers – Lily Broadhead and Gertrude Cowley – in 1921. At first, women officers served in a separate department and specialised in areas of police work associated with women and children, but this segregation was abolished in 1976, since when women officers have been represented in all branches of police activity.

1

THE
CANAL BOAT MURDER

The Murder of Christina Collins on the Trent
and Mersey Canal
June 1839

Christina Brown was born in Notting-
ham, the daughter of an inventor of machines for lace-making and for
the manufacture of fishing nets. The trade of inventor was a precarious
one, and although the family had at one time been prosperous, they
were on parish relief by the time of Christina's father's death in 1818.
Her mother was forced to find work as a nurse, and continued nursing
until she was past 60.

Christina married an older man, Thomas Ingleby, a popular stage
magician known as 'The Emperor of all the Conjurors'. He lived a
nomadic life, touring the country and performing at theatres throughout
the land. His stage show was not for the squeamish. One of his feats
was to slaughter a chicken on stage by cutting off its head, pass the
bloody head among the audience to prove its authenticity, then
miraculously resurrect the bird (actually a second chicken) and send it
strutting around the stage. He would perform a less callous version of
this trick in which he borrowed a pocket watch from a member of the
audience, pounded it into pieces, then restored it to its original
condition before returning it to its owner. He also included an act
involving the devouring of knives and forks.

Christina joined her husband on his travels and became part of his
act, adding singing and dancing to the performance, and later taking
part in the conjuring tricks. The couple had no children. When Thomas
Ingleby died in 1832, he left an attractive young widow aged 30. A few
years later Christina fell in love with Robert Collins, a man of her own
age. The couple married in 1838 and moved to Liverpool to find work.

Christina found a position as a seamstress in the house of a Mrs Grice, but Robert was less successful. In 1839, Robert went to London to seek work, and his luck seemed to improve. Within a week, he had found work as an ostler and taken lodgings in Edgware Road. Immediately he sent a guinea to his wife and asked her to join him in London. Christina was delighted and made her farewells to her employer. She put on her blue silk bonnet, and set out on the long journey.

She did not have enough money to travel by stage coach or on the newly opened railway, and she took the cheaper but slower alternative. She made her way to the northern end of the Trent and Mersey Canal at Preston Brook, and paid the 16-shilling fare to travel to London on a boat belonging to Pickford and Co. The captain of the boat on which Christina embarked was James Owen, and the crew consisted of two men, George Thomas and William Ellis, and a boy, William Musson.

At 7.30 pm on Saturday 15th June, the boat set off. The route to London should have led through Stoke-on-Trent and Rugeley to Fradley junction, where the boat would take the Coventry Canal and continue via Oxford. However, the boat had not travelled far before Christina began to have trouble from the rough – and often drunken – crew. They obviously found the petite and handsome 37 year old woman a subject of lecherous fantasy, and took pleasure in telling her so. When the boat reached Stoke-on-Trent at midday on Sunday, Christina complained to William Brookes, a Pickford's porter, about the behaviour of the men.

Christina also enquired about the possibility of continuing her journey from Stoke by stage coach, but found that no suitable coaches were available. Reluctantly she rejoined the boat and its unpleasant crew. William Brookes' wife travelled on the boat with Christina Collins for the next three and a half miles, and the crew kept their conduct under relative control, but when Mrs Brookes got off Christina was alone with the men again. At Stone, she complained to a Trent and Mersey check clerk that the crew were so drunk that she was frightened that they intended to 'meddle with her'. The clerk advised the distressed passenger to report the men's misconduct when she reached her destination.

Christina decided to walk by herself along the towpath for a while, intending to get back on board when the men were more sober. At the lock-keeper's cottage at Aston, she was seen sharpening a penknife on some stone steps. When the boat arrived, one of the crew was heard shouting abuse at her. However, she had no choice but to rejoin the boat, and was seen to refuse a drink proffered by James Owen, the captain.

At about 9 pm, another Pickford's boat passed, and its captain exchanged words with James Owen. In vulgar language, Owen described what he would like to be doing with his female passenger that night, adding that if he didn't get his way, he would kill her. The terrified woman was seen taking another solitary walk along the towpath at 10 pm by another boat captain.

At midnight, the lock-keeper at Hoo Mill, near Rugeley, was awakened by a woman screaming. He and his wife looked through their window and saw three men by a boat. A woman was sitting on top of the cabin, crying, 'I will not go down. Do not attempt me!' The lock-keeper's wife asked one of the men who the woman was, and he replied that she was a passenger. He also claimed that the woman's husband was travelling with her.

That was the last sighting of Christina Collins alive. Her dead body was found in the canal at Brindley Bank near Rugeley at 5 am the next morning by a boatman, Thomas Grant. She was floating face down in the canal, on the opposite side of the canal from the towpath. Grant stopped his canal boat and used a hook to tow the body over to the towpath. With a passer-by, John Johnson, he got the body out of the water and took it to the Talbot Inn in Rugeley. The dead woman, who was wearing no shoes and no bonnet, was still warm when taken from the canal. Her face was completely black.

When the Pickford agent heard of these events, he sent for the police, and the drunken crew were arrested by a constable when the boat reached Fazeley. Following a coroner's inquest held at the Talbot Inn, the boatmen were charged with the rape and murder of Christina Collins, and sent to the county gaol in Stafford to await trial. The boy, William Musson, was originally charged along with the three adult members of the crew but he was released without charge before the trial.

The original trial was held in July before Mr Justice Williams. The prosecution outlined the rape charge first, but the judge ruled that there was no evidence that the men had raped the victim, and ordered the jury to bring in a verdict of not guilty. The prosecution asked the judge to postpone the trial for murder until a witness who had shared a cell with Owen could be approached. The judge agreed, and the case was put back until the next assizes.

At the second trial, the three boatmen, James Owen, George Thomas

Contemporary newspaper illustrations of the trial of James Owen, George Thomas and William Ellis, and of the execution of Owen and Thomas. (Staffordshire Police Museum)

(sometimes known as Dobell) and William Ellis (sometimes known as Lambert), were jointly charged with the murder of Christina Collins by casting her into the canal, causing her to drown. William Brookes gave evidence of what he had heard and seen at Stoke-on-Trent, where Mrs Collins had complained about the men's behaviour. Brookes said that it was his opinion that the crew had been helping themselves to the spirits in the boat's cargo. He recalled hearing Christina say to Thomas, 'Leave me alone. I'll not have anything to do with you.' Brookes stated that Thomas had replied in foul and abusive language.

Hugh Cordwell, a Trent and Mersey Canal Company check clerk

based at Stone, told the court that when Christina had informed him of her fear of the crew, he had noted that the captain, James Owen, was particularly drunk. John Tansley, an assistant clerk to the Canal Company, said that Christina Collins had arrived at Aston Lock on foot, walking along the towpath. Owen's boat arrived a little later at about 8.30 pm and Christina had rejoined the boat. He had heard one of the crew verbally abuse her and had seen Owen offer her a drink, which she refused.

Thomas Blore, captain of another Pickford's boat, gave evidence that he had exchanged words with Owen when their boats passed at about 9 pm on the Saturday night. Owen had been very crude about his female passenger, describing what he would like to do to her, and saying that if he didn't get his way he would 'burke' her. Blore said that he took this to be a reference to Burke and Hare, who would kill their victims and then sell their bodies for medical research.

A second canal boat captain, Robert Walker, informed the court that, shortly after seeing a woman walking along the towpath, he had met Owen's boat. One of the crew – he was unsure which – had asked him if he'd seen a woman walking by the canal, and described in vulgar detail what he would like to do to her. This was at about 10 o'clock.

The willingness of many of these witnesses to give evidence against fellow boatmen may well have been due to their underlying feelings of guilt. They had ignored Christina Collins's frequent appeals for help, or simply advised her to complain at the end of her journey. They must have seen the distress she was in and they could have given her more assistance, though of course they could not have guessed how far matters would eventually go.

James Mills stated that he and his wife Anne were asleep at Hoo Mill Lock on the night in question. They were woken by screams at midnight, and looking out had seen the three men by the boat and a woman sitting on the cabin roof shouting. Mills said that his wife had asked the men who the woman was, and had been told that she was a passenger and that her husband was accompanying her.

Lock-keeper John Lee said that when Owen's boat reached Woodend Lock, near King's Bromley, early on Monday morning, the captain had reported that a 'deranged' woman passenger had drowned herself. Lee added that Owen was drunk and shaking. However, John Bladon told the court that Owen had not reported the loss of his passenger when the boat had passed through Rugeley, as would have been his duty under company rules.

Standing by the gravestone of murder victim Christina Collins in Rugeley churchyard are her two great-great-great-nephews Trevor and Roy Brown. The two men are direct descendants of Christina's brother Alfred Brown. (John Godwin)

Evidence was given by Samuel Barratt, a local surgeon, that he had examined Christina's body at the Talbot Inn, Rugeley, and had concluded that death was due to suffocation and drowning. He had noted two bruises on her right arm. Hannah Phillips and Elizabeth Matthews stated that they had removed the clothes from the dead woman. They had noticed that the calico drawers were ripped across the front, and one sleeve and cuff of Christina's gown were also torn.

Robert Collins, the husband of the victim, gave his evidence in tears, telling how he had identified his wife's body by a birthmark on her ear.

James Orgill said that he had shared a cell with Owen in Stafford gaol, and the captain had told him that it was Thomas and Ellis who had killed Christina Collins. Musson, the boy member of the crew, told the court that he had been in bed at the time of the murder, and he had heard Ellis snoring. Neither of these witnesses made much impression on the jury however, and a verdict of guilty was pronounced against all three men.

The judge, Mr Baron Gurney, sentenced the three men to death by hanging, saying that the case was one of the most shocking he had ever heard. A helpless and unoffending woman had been under their protection but had become first the object of their lust, and then, to avoid detection, the object of their cruelty. He advised them not to look for pardon in this world, but to prepare themselves for an ignominious death.

An appeal on behalf of William Ellis was presented to the Secretary of State, pointing out that the evidence showed him to be less involved in the crime than his companions. As a result, the death sentence in his case was commuted to transportation for life; this news was given to him as the three condemned were taking their final Sacrament from the prison chaplain. As a result of a report from the governor of Stafford prison, the sentence against Ellis was further reduced from life to 14 years and he was sent to Australia.

Owen and Thomas paid the ultimate price for the murder, and were hanged in front of Stafford gaol on 11th April 1840. Ten thousand spectators attended the event, many regarding it as an exciting day's entertainment to be accompanied by much drinking and merry-making. As was common at public hangings, the local pickpockets found it a wonderfully rewarding occasion to practise their trade, despite the fact that theft was itself a hanging offence!

The hangman was William Calcraft, who made a good living by conducting provincial hangings at £10 a time. His assistant should have been Tom Cheshire, but he had spent the night before drinking at the Shoulder of Mutton, and failed to turn up. The hangman needed an assistant, because the drop at that time was a short one, not sufficient to break the condemned man's neck. It was the assistant's task to go below the staging and hasten death by pulling on the hanged man's legs. Calcraft appealed to the governor of the prison, and a prisoner was found willing to take up a new career. George Smith became the hangman's assistant, and learned his trade so well that he eventually became a hangman in his own right, officiating at the execution of the notorious Dr Palmer (see Chapter 2).

TWO
DEADLY DOCTORS

The Murder of John Wood at Burslem,
and of John Parsons Cook at Rugeley
January 1797 and November 1855

The elderly Dr Hickman, who had a practice in Burslem in the 1790s, employed a young assistant, Dr Thomas Milward Oliver, to take on some of his patients. One of the families the new doctor visited was that of a wealthy pottery owner, John Wood. The Wood family lived in a large house on a country estate between Burslem and Tunstall, close to their pottery factory.

Dr Oliver was originally called in to attend to the ailing Mrs Wood, but it was Maria Wood, the pretty daughter of the family, who caught his attention. Tom fell in love with her, and it soon became clear that Maria was just as fond of the tall young doctor. At first, John Wood tolerated the friendship, but when it became obvious that the young couple were thinking in terms of marriage, he decided that the romantic liaison must be brought to an abrupt end. To a modern observer, a handsome young doctor might sound like an acceptable 'catch', but in the late 18th century this was certainly not so. A wealthy family such as the Woods would have much higher expectations of a suitable son-in-law. John Wood was not going to have Maria marry a lowly doctor, with no money behind him. Tom Oliver was banned from entering the house, and Maria was forbidden to see him.

The couple did not see each other for 12 months, but their feelings for each other remained intense. After a chance meeting in the summer of 1796, Tom and Maria began to meet secretly at an old water mill on the Wood family estate. When John Wood learned of his daughter's disobedience, he was furious. He surprised them at their trysting place,

The Rugeley home of Dr William Palmer. (John Godwin)

and lost his temper. An angry exchange of words between Dr Oliver and Maria's father developed into an exchange of blows.

Following this incident, John Wood kept an even stricter eye on his daughter's activities, and the couple were again unable to meet. Tom began to spend his evenings in the Turk's Head Inn, brooding. When acquaintances began to tease him about his love for Maria, suggesting that it was her money he was after, he grew angry and resentful.

Then, in late December, Mrs Wood became ill again and sent for Dr Oliver. This surprising decision was no doubt made because she had been impressed by her earlier treatment from the young doctor, but it must surely indicate that she did not share her husband's disapproval of Maria's suitor. Whatever her motives, the consequence was that Tom Oliver began to see Maria again whenever he went to attend Mrs Wood. However, their meetings were only at the house in the presence of others, and Tom Oliver still burned with bitterness against Maria's father.

One of Tom's drinking companions at the Turk's Head was Ralph Johnson. Ralph was a keen pistol-shooter and he introduced Tom Oliver to his hobby. On the evening of 26th January, Dr Oliver borrowed two pistols from his friend and took them home. The next morning, a Friday, Dr Oliver presented himself at the Wood family home and demanded to see John Wood. He received a curt reply that Mr Wood was unavailable and that he was to see Mr Bathman, the chief clerk, who would pay his bill. Dr Oliver went to the clerk's office, but he insisted that his business was personal and with Mr Wood.

Eventually, John Wood came to the office. According to evidence given later by Mr Bathman, Dr Oliver raised one of the pistols and shot John Wood in the chest. Tom Oliver was seized before he could use the second pistol, but he managed to put a large dose of poison into his mouth, saying that he would never leave the house alive. However, he immediately vomited out the poison, and when John Wood died of his chest wound three days later, Dr Oliver was charged with his murder.

Despite his defence that he had gone to the Wood home that morning intending to commit suicide in front of John Wood, he was found guilty. The court rejected his plea that he had been provoked into shooting when Mr Wood had sneered at his lowly status and poor income. A later plea of insanity was ignored, and Dr Thomas Oliver was sentenced to death. He was hanged at a public execution in Stafford.

*   *   *

Notorious though the Dr Oliver case was, Staffordshire's most well-known murderous physician was Dr William Palmer. William, born in Rugeley in 1824, was the second of five brothers. They were a mixed lot: Joseph was a wealthy merchant, George a solicitor, and Thomas an Anglican clergyman, but Walter became a bankrupt alcoholic. William himself eventually became a doctor, but only after a very unsavoury start to his career.

After attending Rugeley Grammar School, where he had the reputation of being a spendthrift of money he had borrowed, he was apprenticed to Evans & Sons, a firm of wholesale chemists in Liverpool. While he was there he seduced the daughter of the family with whom he lodged. This young lady was the first in a long line of William's conquests, as seduction was a favourite leisure activity that was to become a lifelong interest. However, it was embezzlement rather than sexual adventuring that led to his dismissal. He was caught opening the firm's letters and stealing money. William had spent the stolen money on ladies of the night and betting on horses, but his widowed mother made good the missing money, thus preventing him being taken to court and charged. Evans & Sons were obviously satisfied with this arrangement as they allowed William's brother Thomas to take over the apprenticeship in his place.

William returned to Staffordshire and began a career in medicine by being apprenticed to Dr Edward Tylecote in Great Haywood. He made a point of attending church regularly, but arranged to be frequently called out of the service to attend a sick patient. In reality, he was visiting his young mistress, Jane Widnall, while her parents remained safely in the church he had just left. At Great Haywood, he again practised his dishonest habits, cheating patients out of their money. Once again, his mother had to restore money he had stolen.

William next took up work at Stafford Infirmary, and was suspected of poisoning a man named Abley, who had challenged him to a drinking competition. Although nothing was proved, the infirmary brought in a new order forbidding students to enter the dispensary where the poisons were kept.

In 1846, William was sent to complete his training under Dr Stegall in London. While in the metropolis, William lived a wild life of partying, gambling and womanising. One anxious hospital official refused to give William lodgings in his house, stating that he had the moral welfare of his daughters to consider. Given William's extravagant and licentious lifestyle, it is somewhat surprising that he succeeded in completing his medical training and gained the Diploma of the College of Surgeons. It may be less surprising that he failed to pay Dr Stegall the 50 guineas he had promised him for helping him pass his exams!

Dr Palmer returned to his native Rugeley and set up practice in a house in Market Street. He soon began to pay court to an 18 year old girl named Ann Brookes, who lived with her guardian, Charles Dawson, in Abbot's Bromley. Ann had been left a considerable sum of money by her late father, a colonel in the Indian Army, which may well have been why William decided that on this occasion he would marry the girl. Despite Charles Dawson's misgivings, Ann fell for the blandishments of William Palmer, who could charm the birds off the trees if he set his mind to it. William and Ann were married at the village church in Abbot's Bromley in October 1847.

William Palmer had always been fond of horse-racing, and now – in spite of the fact that his medical practice was not making him much money – he established a stable of race-horses, and arranged for them to be trained in Hednesford. His racing enterprises lost money continuously, and Dr Palmer's debts grew larger.

A year after her marriage, Ann Palmer gave birth to a son. Four later children all died as babies, and their nurse, Ann Bradshaw, stated publicly that she believed that Dr Palmer had killed them by putting sugar laced with poison on his finger for them to suck, because he could not afford to provide for them.

Other people connected with William Palmer also died unexpectedly, including his illegitimate child, who died shortly after being examined by Dr Palmer. Palmer's mother-in-law died while visiting Palmer, immediately after lending him money. Mr Bladon of Ashby-de-la-Zouch visited Dr Palmer in May 1850 to collect some debts; he died during the visit and was buried very promptly. While at a race meeting, Dr Palmer gave medical attention to Mr Bly of Norfolk, to whom he owed £800. When Bly died, Palmer denied owing the money and told the dead man's wife that the debt was owed the other way, to himself.

It was at about this time that William Palmer insured his wife's life for £13,000. When she was taken ill in 1854, Dr Palmer asked an 80 year old colleague, Dr Bamford, to attend her, but he also continued to prescribe for her himself. Ann Palmer died, and her death was recorded as being caused by cholera. Although William appeared to mourn his wife's death, shedding many tears at her funeral, it has to be noted that the 18 year old housemaid, Eliza Tharme, bore him an illegitimate child just nine months after Ann's death. The baby was born in Dr Palmer's house but died six months later.

The £13,000 insurance money from Ann's death was soon dissipated, and William tried to insure his brother Walter for £80,000. The insurance companies were suspicious of this large sum, and the eventual sum assured was considerably smaller. Even so, when Walter Palmer died very soon after the insurance was taken out, the company refused to pay. When Palmer tried to insure the life of a friend, George Bate, he could find no company willing to accept the proposal.

William was now desperate to obtain money. Apart from his many debts, he was being blackmailed by Jane Bergen, a young lady with whom he had had a torrid affair. Jane was threatening to show his love letters to her father, a Stafford policeman. These love letters, now stored at Stafford County Record Office, are very frank and salacious, referring frequently to the couple's sexual activities.

One of Dr Palmer's racing cronies was John Parsons Cook of Lutterworth. Like Palmer, Cook was a professional man – he had trained as a solicitor – who preferred to spend his time and money at the racecourse. When one of Cook's horses won the Shrewsbury Handicap, it netted him £1,700, a sum which the impecunious Dr

Palmer eyed covetously. After a celebration party in a Shrewsbury hotel, the two men returned to Rugeley. Cook took a room in the Talbot Arms Hotel, which was situated opposite Palmer's house.

Dr Palmer invited John to dinner, but after the meal the visitor was taken violently ill. The next day, William sent his sick friend some broth but he was unable to eat it. A chambermaid thought it a pity to waste the broth and drank some, but it caused her to be sick too. Palmer sent for the elderly Dr Bamford again, who prescribed some pills for John Cook. Palmer took pains to draw attention to the handwriting on the pill box, commenting on Dr Bamford's beautiful script. During the night Cook became desperately ill again, shrieking and having convulsions until his body contorted into a rigid curve. He died in agony. William Palmer certified that his friend had died from apoplexy, and arranged for the body to be laid out immediately.

When Cook's stepfather, William Stevens, arrived from Lutterworth, he suspected that Dr Palmer had removed money and papers from the dead man. At the post-mortem, Cook's intestines and stomach were pronounced 'healthy' but Stevens insisted that the organs be sent to London for further analysis. The driver of the carriage engaged to transport the jar containing the organs was to claim later that Palmer offered him a bribe of £10 to upset the jar.

Palmer became very anxious to know the result of the second analysis of Cook's stomach, and bribed the Rugeley postmaster Samuel Cheshire to open the letter from London containing the result. When he read that no poison had been found, William Palmer said, 'I knew it. I'm as innocent as a baby.'

When the Rugeley coroner received a gift of poultry from Dr Palmer, this was seen as another bribe. The inquest heard that Dr Palmer had bought strychnine just before Cook's death and, despite the absence of poison in the corpse, a verdict of wilful murder was brought in.

William Palmer was arrested, and an order was made for the exhumation of his late wife and his brother. Their bodies were examined by Dr Alfred Taylor of Guy's Hospital; he concluded that Ann had probably died of antimony poisoning, though the evidence in the case of Walter Palmer was inconclusive.

However, it was for the murder of John Parsons Cook that Dr Palmer was tried. He should have been tried in Stafford, but because of the strong feelings against Palmer in Staffordshire, the Lord Chancellor brought in a bill to enable offenders to be tried away from the scene of their alleged crime, in certain circumstances. This bill was passed and became known as the Palmer Act; it is still in force.

The trial of Dr William Palmer was therefore held at the Old Bailey in London, where the prosecution was led by the Attorney General himself. The top medical men of the country were called on to give evidence on one side or the other. All of the evidence against Palmer was circumstantial, the prosecution case resting on the similarity between the symptoms shown by Cook as he died and those known to be caused by strychnine poisoning. Although the medical witnesses gave differing opinions of the cause of John Cook's death, Sir Benjamin Brodie, the president of the Royal College of Surgeons, stated tha Cook's symptoms were unlike any form of natural disease anc indicated that he had been given strychnine. This evidence, togethei with the fact that Dr Palmer had purchased strychnine before Cook's death, weighed heavily on the jury. After a 12-day trial, William Palmer was found guilty of murder and sentenced by the judge, Lord Chief Justice Campbell, to be taken back to Stafford to be hanged in public.

Palmer maintained his innocence to the last, refusing attempts by the prison chaplain to persuade him to confess for the good of his soul. His brother, the Rev Thomas Palmer, petitioned for a reprieve on the grounds that it was wrong to hang a man on purely circumstantial evidence, but these moves failed.

At 8 am on Saturday 14th June 1856, William Palmer was taken out to the scaffold, which had been erected outside Stafford prison. Crowds had been gathering since 3 am; some were local people, though a sizeable number had travelled to Stafford by train, by carriage, on horseback or on foot. Some were still under the influence of the previous night's heavy drinking in the local hostelries. Nonconformist preachers were handing out religious tracts, and there were several placards carried aloft with biblical texts written on them. Others were there just for the entertainment, the spectacle, the thrill of being at such an important public event. In all, the crowd numbered over 30,000 people. The more well-to-do had managed to get themselves a good viewpoint on balconies and raised platforms; some carried telescopes.

Palmer took his place in the grim procession, which included the Chief Constable, the high sheriff, the prison governor and the chaplain. The condemned man was bare-headed, and wore a coarse jacket provided by the prison. He appeared the most calm person present. He climbed the steps of the scaffold to meet a man dressed in a white smock and top hat. This was hangman George Smith, a former inmate of Stafford prison, who had volunteered to act as assistant hangman at

A reconstruction of William Palmer's face taken from his death mask. (John Godwin)

the execution of Owen and Thomas 16 years earlier, and had since worked his way up to the position of official hangman.

William Palmer shook hands with Smith, who then proceeded to place the rope around the doctor's neck, and a white hood over his face. The bolt was drawn and Palmer dropped to his death. He was 31 years of age. His mother, who knew her son's vices only too well, never accepted his guilt on the murder charge. Her comment on his death was, 'They have hanged my saintly Billy.' Some scholars agreed with her; Robert Graves is one who believes that the doctor's appalling record as an embezzler, womaniser and reckless gambler made the public willing to believe him capable of – and guilty of – murder, even though there was no real evidence that Cook had been murdered.

There is one wry footnote to the case. After the Palmer case, a number of eminent Rugeley men became disturbed that the name of their town would always be associated with 'Palmer the Poisoner'. They petitioned the prime minister of the day to ask whether Rugeley could be known by a different name. The prime minister – a man not previously known for his sense of humour – replied that he was prepared to allow their request but only if the town could be named after him. The good burghers considered this alternative – Palmerston – and decided that they could live with the name Rugeley after all!

3

'POVERTY,
POVERTY KNOCK'

The murder of Elizabeth Gould at Alstonfield, *1811;*
of William Cooper at Halmerend, *1844;*
of Thomas Smith at Whiston, *1866;*
of Thomas Brough at Biddulph, *1845;*
and of George Walker at Audley, *1864*

The case of John Gould, tried in 1811 for the murder of his wife Elizabeth, is one of rural poverty and desperation. Gould was a 23 year old farm worker living in the north Staffordshire village of Alstonfield. He was described as having a face that expressed youthful rusticity, rather than hardness of mind. John lived an impecunious, hand-to-mouth existence, and found it near impossible to earn enough to provide for his family. When Elizabeth told her husband that she was expecting their second child, the couple were at the end of their tether.

Together they planned to abort the pregnancy in the crudest possible way. John rolled on his pregnant wife and elbowed her repeatedly in the abdomen. When Elizabeth died of her injuries, her heartbroken young husband was arrested.

The court might have been inclined to take the pathetic situation into account, but John's two sisters made things worse by perjuring themselves with a story that the bruises on Elizabeth's body had been caused when a stone wall collapsed on her. This attempt to subvert the course of justice annoyed the court and may have had the opposite effect to that which the sisters intended. The jury took a long while to arrive at their verdict, but when they did, it was to find John Gould guilty of his wife's murder. When he was sentenced to death, he cried out, 'I am murdered!'

Contemporary accounts of his public execution indicate that he did not face death bravely, being dragged to the gallows in tears. The spectators were – for once – sympathetic to the man on the gibbet.

*   *   *

Rural poverty and the necessity to put food on the family table led many men into poaching. The sworn enemies of the poaching fraternity were the village policeman and the gamekeeper.

William Cooper was the 23 year old son of a gamekeeper. A labourer by day, he would help his father Tom to protect the game on the estate of Sir T F F Boughey at night. Tom and Will Cooper lived in an isolated house called The Hays on the edge of the wood at Halmerend, near Audley. One Sunday evening in August 1844, Will had been to chapel in Audley but had stopped for a pint of beer at the King's Head on his way home – an interesting combination of leisure pursuits, to say the least! When he reached The Hays, he was about to open the door when a gun was discharged. A load of small shot hit him in the throat, choking his cries and felling him to the ground.

His father was roused from his bed by the sound of the gunfire, and rushed down to find Will lying half-in the doorway of the house. Tom took his son in his arms, and held him as the boy breathed his last. The police arrived the next day, and discovered two sets of footprints in the mud close to the house. Major McKnight followed the tracks over the fields to Scot Hay.

Later that day, he arrested a collier named Paul Downing, who had just been released from prison after serving a two-month term for 'trespassing in search of game'. At his trial, Downing had said that the evidence against him given by Tom Cooper was false, and when he was found guilty, he uttered threats of vengeance against the keeper. Major McKnight demanded to examine Paul Downing's boots, and an unusual arrangement of nails on the heels was found to correspond with the footprints left near the murder scene.

Downing denied being near the Coopers' house on the Sunday night, saying that he had been staying with his 17 year old cousin, Charles Powys, at Scot Hay. When Powys was questioned about his cousin's alibi, his own boots were examined and found to match the second set of footprints discovered by the police. The police searched his house and, under some clothing in a drawer, they found a shotgun which had been recently fired and a powder horn plugged with blue paper.

Similar blue paper had been found near the keeper's house, and the two cousins were charge with the murder of Will Cooper.

At the trial, surgeon Hugh Davis gave the court evidence of his findings at the post-mortem. Will Cooper had received shot wounds to the throat, face and chest. His carotid artery had been severed, causing him to haemorrhage internally. Death would have occurred a few minutes after the shot was fired.

Police Constable Tom Basford gave evidence that he had heard Paul Downing swearing to get even with Cooper, whom he accused of giving false evidence against him, causing him to be imprisoned for poaching. PC Basford said that Downing had not mentioned Cooper's Christian name, and he did not know whether it was the father or son who was being threatened. He thought that Downing was 'in a great passion and in haste', and he could not say whether he really intended to do the keepers any bodily harm.

Paul Downing and Charles Powys continued to protest their innocence of the murder, but both men were found guilty. As the court could not decide which man had fired the shot, both were sentenced to death by public hanging. The death sentence was carried out on 4th January 1845. On the gallows, Downing proclaimed, 'We are going to die for a thing we know nothing about and I hope the Lord in heaven will protect us.' He also prophesied: 'It will be known before 12 months who is the guilty man.' Downing died immediately, but his young cousin took several minutes. After the execution, there were many rumours of another man confessing to the murder, but the authorities denied that there was any truth in the reports, putting them down to the public-house ramblings of a drunken man.

*   *   *

Another poacher to die on the scaffold was William Collier, and he was hanged twice! He was found guilty of murdering Thomas Smith of Whiston, near Cheadle. When Thomas's dead body was found in a wood called the Black Planting, the whole locality was in an uproar. The dead man was no ordinary keeper; he was the son of Thomas Smith senior, the lord of the manor of Whiston Eaves, and therefore a man of some status.

The younger Thomas often used to go out at night with the gamekeepers, keeping a vigilant eye out for poachers. On the night of Wednesday 4th July 1866, he had been out with keeper James Bamford in the locality known as Moneystone Common, near the village of Cotton. In order to cover a wide area, the two men had positioned themselves about a mile apart. However, when Thomas failed to turn up at the prearranged meeting place the next morning, a search party was instigated. At Quarry Hole, the searchers found clothing and other items belonging to Thomas, and at 9.30 am they discovered his body, lying in a hollow in the nearby wood.

Thomas Smith had been shot, and then battered about the head. It seemed that the blows that had fractured his skull had been caused by a gunstock, and a ramrod was found near the body. His hat, which poignantly still bore a wild rose he had put there the previous day, had been peppered with shot.

The authorities had a good idea where to look for the culprit, and the next day they arrested William Collier, a known local poacher. Collier had seven children, and the meat he obtained from his nocturnal poaching formed a large part of his family's diet. A shotgun was found hidden in a drain near Collier's home, with dark hair adhering to the stock. Mr Mellor of Hollington identified the gun as one he had sold to William Collier; he also identified its ramrod, found near the dead man's body.

At William Collier's trial, surgeon Thomas Webb from Cheadle gave evidence that he had examined Collier's clothing on Saturday 7th July and had found bloodstains on his collar and trousers.

Collier was found guilty of the crime, and, despite the jury's recommendation to mercy, he was sentenced to be hanged. On 7th August, a crowd gathered outside Stafford gaol and the condemned man was brought to the scaffold. However, the hangman was not on his best form: when the trapdoor opened, William Collier dropped through it followed by the entire rope, which had not been correctly attached to the beam! A bemused Collier was brought out from beneath the platform, and to the loudly expressed annoyance of the crowd, who were by now thoroughly on the side of the prisoner, the whole procedure began again. This time, the hangman made sure of his knots and William Collier died.

*   *   *

Another man affected by money problems was John Brough of Whitefields Farm, Biddulph. He lived with his mother – who was the actual tenant of the farm – and his young nephew. By the beginning of

1845, the family were having trouble finding the rent, and the landlord was pressing them to pay up. The fact that the landlord lived on the neighbouring High Bent Farm, and was John's brother, Thomas, made no difference to their plight. The rent was in arrears, and Thomas Brough wanted it paid. Thomas was not a subscriber to the blood-is-thicker-than-water sentiment at all. In fact, his own sister described him as 'a selfish and unprincipled man'. The local constable said that Thomas was 'rather rough and angry when put up ... a hot-headed man. The family seemed afraid of him as a man who had power over them.'

This constable, Thomas Mitchell, was one of the bailiffs instructed by Thomas Brough to go to Whitefields on Friday 3rd January to collect the £29 12s owing to him. Old Mrs Brough was heartbroken that her son should treat his family so cruelly, and she asked the bailiffs to send someone to High Bent to beg Thomas to come and settle the matter in a friendly manner.

The bailiffs were sympathetic to her request, and Thomas duly arrived, still demanding his money. His mother went on her knees, begging him to give them time to send a pig to market to raise some money. Her hard-hearted son ignored her. In the words of Constable Mitchell, Thomas Brough simply 'passed her by and said nothing'.

Thomas obviously felt that the bailiffs had not carried out his instructions correctly, and later that day, he went to Whitefields on his own. There he seized two boxes of goods belonging to John and another brother, James, intending to sell them to make good the debt. As he carried them back to his own farm, John accompanied him, begging him not to take the goods away. He promised that the debt would be settled in full if only Thomas would give them longer to pay.

Thomas refused to listen at first, but then said that he would consider the request the next day. John had some doubts about this, especially when Thomas began to speak about getting papers drawn up to sell the stock of Whitefields. As the two brothers walked along, John noticed a hammer leaning against a stone wall and he picked it up. As Thomas Brough coldly refused to listen to his brother's entreaties, John struck him one blow on the head. The injured man stood for a while, then fell down. John returned to his farm in a state of turmoil, throwing the hammer into a field on the way.

Back at High Bent Farm, Thomas's wife Hannah had returned from selling butter in Tunstall and began to prepare her husband's supper. When he had not returned by 6 o'clock, she sent out a young farmhand to look for him. The lad was about 16 and very nervous. When he was about halfway between the two farms, he heard a groaning coming from 20 yards or so away. There was a rustling in the hedge, and something was dragging itself along the ground. Convinced that a boggart – a ghost – was coming for him, the lad returned to the farm, but did not tell Hannah Brough what he had heard.

Back at Whitefields, John had done a few jobs around the farm but was unable to settle. He decided to go back and see whether his brother had got up and gone home. When he reached the place where he had struck Thomas, he saw him on a slope beside a water-filled ditch. John was relieved to see that Thomas was sitting up. However, when he heard another person approach – it was, of course, the lad from High Bent Farm – John hid. When he heard a splash from the ditch, John thought that the unknown person nearby would find Thomas and help him. John went home to wash, then set out to visit his brother James.

John told James that Thomas had taken his property to sell, and asked James to accompany him to High Bent to see if Thomas was there. He did so, and was told by Hannah that Thomas had not been seen. As they walked away, John broke down into tears and said that he thought he would be hanged. He confessed that he had struck Thomas with a hammer. He said that he thought Thomas must be dead, and he begged James to go and look for him. Terrified, James refused and went back to his home.

John returned to Whitefields and sat by the fire all night. At 5 o'clock the next morning, he went back to the meadow where he had left Thomas and found his body lying with its feet on the bank and the head and shoulders in the water. He pulled the body out of the ditch and carried it some distance to Gledelow sand pit. He put the body of his brother on the edge, and allowed it to roll down into the pit.

The body was spotted the next day by John Shufflebotham, a labourer from Biddulph, who ran to the Talbot Arms and raised the alarm. The body was recovered, and a post-mortem was conducted by surgeon John Harrison of Burslem. He found wounds on both sides of the head, and beneath the wound on the left side, the skull had been fractured. He stated that death had been instantaneous.

A search for the murder weapon was instigated, and the blood-stained hammer was found in a meadow belonging to Whitefields Farm. John and James Brough were arrested, but James was released soon afterwards.

At John Brough's trial, his young nephew identified the hammer as one used on the farm to break stones. Evidence was given by James Brough, who told the court what John had confessed when he called on him on the Friday night. In his own evidence, John Brough told the court how he had struck Thomas with the hammer, adding, 'I declare most solemnly, I did not intend to kill my brother, or even strike him, ten minutes before I did so.' The jury found him guilty, but recommended mercy because of the man's previous good character. As commonly happened, the judge ignored the jury's recommendation and sentenced John Brough to death. He was hanged before a crowd of 600 spectators, a relatively small turn-out for a public execution.

The contradiction between the instantaneous-death verdict of the coroner and John's account of seeing his brother sitting up some time after the blow remains a mystery, as does the second blow to the skull. When the young lad from High Bent Farm heard Thomas groaning and dragging himself along the ditch, he was obviously still alive. It is just possible that another of Thomas Brough's enemies – and he had several – found the injured man and finished him off, leaving John to pay the ultimate penalty.

*   *   *

In 1864, John Brough's nephew Charles also met death on the gallows. Charles Brough – a diabetic who found it difficult to walk – was charged with the murder of 75 year old George Walker.

George lived in a small hut in a quarry near Audley, and scratched a living by cultivating the land around his home. In his day he had been a tenant farmer, but in later years, thanks largely to his generosity to friends, he had fallen on hard times. His wooden home measured only 5ft by 6ft, and was only 4ft high, being roofed with turf. The floor was bare earth, and George's bed was a board covered in hay. He had few possessions, but he did own a pocket watch of which he was immensely proud, and a knife with a broken tip.

On the day before his death, George had walked into Audley to visit his brother-in-law Ralph Warburton, and had asked for a loan of 6d. Ralph, obviously another generous member of the family, had actually given him 2s 6d. George had been visited by his friend, John Northrop, that evening and the two men had enjoyed a convivial chat, discussing the news of the day.

When John came back the next day, Thursday 28th July 1864, he was horrified and heartbroken to find George lying dead outside his hut. He had been battered about the head, and his hut had been broken into. From the bloodstains inside the hut, the police were able to establish that the old man had been attacked while lying in bed. Both the half-crown given him by Ralph Warburton and the pocket watch and its brass chain were missing. John Northrop was able to describe the watch in great detail, since he had bought it five months earlier and had swapped it for a watch owned by his friend. He told the police that it was made of German silver, had Roman figures on the dial, and was marked with the number 45177. John showed the police where George had carved the numbers on the hut's doorframe.

These facts were to prove vital in the apprehension of George Walker's murderer. The next day, a man walked into Hulme's pawnshop in Tunstall and tried to obtain 25 shillings for a pocket watch. The assistant in the pawnshop, James Jones, became suspicious. He made an excuse to go out of the shop, leaving the customer still waiting inside. Minutes later he returned, accompanied by two policemen.

When questioned, the customer initially said that his name was Charles Jones, and he claimed that he had bought the watch from a William Smith three weeks earlier. The two policemen, Sergeant Harrison and PC Cooke, arrested the man and took him back to the police station. When searched he was found to have a knife with a broken tip, and money which included a half-crown. He also had dried blood on his clothing. At this stage he told the police his real name – Charles Brough – and claimed that the items all belonged to his father.

Brough was charged with the murder of George Walker, and later that evening, he made a statement in which he admitted killing the old man. His story was that he had entered the hut, intending to have a rest, since he was suffering with diabetes. However, the old man had been in the hut and had come to the door. Brough said that he had picked up a wooden wheelspoke and hit the man with it twice. He had then taken the watch from his pocket and walked off.

At Charles Brough's trial, the evidence given by surgeon Richard Vernon, who had conducted the post-mortem on the dead man, contradicted Brough's statement. He found that George Walker had been struck 50 or 60 times, both with the wooden wheelspoke and also with a metal bar. He had also been stamped on by a heavy boot. The police were able to prove that Brough's description of the event failed to tally with the extensive bloodstains found inside the hut. The two weapons used in the attack had in fact been taken from inside the hut.

The defence argument that Charles Brough's diabetes had caused him to commit the attack was dismissed by the judge, and the jury brought in a guilty verdict. Charles Brough was publicly hanged 19 years after his uncle had met the same fate. This time, however, a crowd of 8,000 watched the execution, and few of them can have harboured the same sympathy shown by the 600 who watched John Brough hang.

4

THE
HEADLESS WOMAN OF HEDNESFORD

The Murder of Elizabeth Gaskin at Hednesford
February 1919

'**M**eet me round the pool at once – important.' This was the eight-word note written to 23 year old Elizabeth Gaskin by her estranged husband Thomas, on Wednesday 19th February 1919. They were eight words that led Elizabeth to her death.

She was living with her mother at Brindley Heath, Hednesford, and the letter was hand-delivered to the house by Tom Saunders, who worked with Thomas Gaskin at West Cannock colliery. Saunders told Elizabeth that he had been given the note while having a lunchtime drink with Thomas Gaskin in the Anglesey Arms in Hednesford. Elizabeth immediately left her six week old baby with her mother, and set off to walk the short distance to the pool, which was situated near the Cannock & Rugeley colliery offices. Looking through the window, two colliery officials saw Elizabeth and Thomas Gaskin walking towards the nearby wood. They appeared to be quarrelling. The two observers saw the couple part, Thomas climbing over a wire fence and going into the wood, Elizabeth walking away in the opposite direction.

Elizabeth was never seen alive again. When she failed to return from her appointment, her mother notified the police, who organised a search of the wood. Thomas Gaskin was questioned on the Thursday, but denied meeting his wife the day before. As Thursday and Friday went by, other police officers were drafted in, and local reservoirs were dragged.

The police were still convinced that Thomas Gaskin had been responsible for his wife's disappearance, and on Friday afternoon, the police intercepted Gaskin as he was about to begin his 4 pm shift at the

A souvenir postcard issued at the time to commemorate the murder. (Staffordshire Library Service/John Godwin)

colliery. He was taken to Cannock police station for questioning by Superintendent Morrey, and there he again denied meeting his wife on the Wednesday afternoon. He was still at the police station on Sunday when he suddenly requested to speak to Inspector Woolley.

The inspector was sent for, and when he arrived at the police station, Thomas Gaskin made a strange request, asking if it were possible for a search to be made for his wife's body without the Hednesford police knowing about it. When Inspector Woolley replied that it would be possible, Gaskin said that he would take him to where the body was hidden. He added ominously, 'You will want two drags and two men to pull the drags in opposite directions. She is in pieces.'

A taxi was summoned to take Gaskin and the police officers back to Hednesford. They went to the gasworks in Victoria Street, where Gaskin led the officers over a 5-ft wall and pointed to the water-filled tank surrounding the base of the gasholder. 'She is there,' he informed them.

A macabre search began. Elizabeth's mutilated and headless body was recovered first, and two days later the head was fished out. Gaskin told the police that he had met up with his wife again minutes after they had been seen parting on Wednesday afternoon. Elizabeth had suggested that they return to her mother's house to discuss their domestic problems. When he refused, Elizabeth had started to cry, and he had seized her by the throat and strangled her.

He had left the body in the wood, but returned some hours later to dismember it. He had managed to cut off the head, but his attempts to hack off the limbs were less successful. His original intention had been to transport the head and torso in a wheelbarrow, but realising that the barrow would leave a track on the snow-covered ground, he left it at the edge of the wood and carried the dismembered corpse the rest of the way in his arms. He had initially put the torso into a culvert, and thrown the head and clothing into the tank under the gasholder. On the Thursday night, after being questioned by the police, he had recovered the headless body from the culvert. Weighting the body down by thrusting a length of gas pipe through it, he cast it into the water where the head had been left the night before.

At Thomas Gaskin's trial, held in Stafford in July 1919, the prosecuting counsel, Mr C K Vachell KC, began by telling the jury, 'I shudder to think I have to present to you a case which is so full of ferocious detail.' He described the injuries to Elizabeth Gaskin's body as 'a gruesome catalogue of the most savage cruelty'.

Evidence was given by the dead woman's mother, Emily Talbot, who told the court that Thomas and Elizabeth had married in 1913, but were living apart by the time Thomas had joined the Royal Engineers in 1916. She said that her daughter had had two children while Thomas was serving in France and that Elizabeth had admitted to her that one of the children was not fathered by Thomas Gaskin. She said that Elizabeth's army allowance had been stopped while an inquiry into her character took place. In spite of this, Thomas Gaskin had been on friendly terms with his wife when he came home on leave, and had been prepared to bring up the children as his own.

Mr Graham Milward KC presented a defence based on Thomas Gaskin's insanity. He claimed that the extraordinary nature of the crime, and the brutality of the manner in which the body was mangled, indicated that the perpetrator could not have been sane at the time of the murder. Gaskin's mother told the court that, as a boy, Thomas had once tried to strangle himself with a scarf. He had always been strange in his manners and this had been worse since his return from the war. Ernest Woodhall and Charles Dawson, two former army comrades of the accused man, told the court of the reckless things Gaskin had done at the front, including going backwards and forwards among flying shells and falling buildings. They said that he had been blown up by a

German mine, and had not been the same since.

Despite the plea of insanity, the jury deliberated for only 14 minutes before returning a verdict of guilty. Thomas Gaskin was sentenced to death, and was hanged at Winson Green prison, Birmingham, on 8th August 1919.

5

CAUGHT
BY THE BBC

The Murder of Charles Fox in West Bromwich
August 1933

The crimes committed by Eric Hobday on the night of Sunday 27th August 1933 revealed him to be a cool customer, ruthless but in some respects incredibly foolish. When, at 4.20 am, he removed the putty from the kitchen window of a house in Moor Street, West Bromwich, he was intending to break in to look for petty cash. This was just one of a number of houses he had burgled that night.

The occupants of the house, Charles and Gladys Fox, had been asleep in bed since 10 o'clock, but when Hobday dropped the pane of glass, Gladys Fox woke up. Alarmed, Gladys woke her husband and told him that someone was in the house. Charles had not had a full-time job for over two years – ironically, he was due to start as a metal worker at Messrs Bagnall of Lee Bridge the next morning – but he had worked as a part-time agent of the National Clothing Company. He knew that there was 14 shillings from his day's doorstep collecting in the house, and he was determined that the intruder should not get it.

Urged on by his wife, Charles Fox lit a candle and came downstairs to investigate, wearing only his vest and underpants. Gladys followed close behind him, leaving their six week old baby still sleeping in his cot.

They had just had time to notice that the kitchen window was open before the candle blew out, plunging them into complete darkness. As Charles went towards the kitchen window, Gladys heard a scuffle and fled back upstairs. The burglar with whom Charles was struggling was a very small man but he was, unfortunately, armed with a sheath knife. Gladys, anxiously waiting upstairs, heard her husband staggering up the stairs, saying, 'He's stabbed me!' She managed to get him onto a bedside chair, but he then fell dead on the floor. To her horror, she saw a knife protruding from his back. Gladys opened the bedroom window and shouted for help. Her terrified screams were heard by a passer-by, Harold Taylor. Taylor alerted the police, and a murder hunt began.

Incredibly, Charles Fox's murderer had left the murder scene only to go into a neighbouring street, Bromford Lane, and break into another house, the home and butcher's shop of a Mr Newton. Here, Eric Hobday had a wash and shave, and drank a pint of milk, before stealing a small amount of money. When Mr Newton discovered he had been burgled, he found his recently used razor lying in a bowl of soapy water. Moreover, he also found that a workbox had been opened and a needle threaded with cotton. The burglar had taken the time to do some running repairs to his clothing.

Eric Hobday was certainly cool and cheeky, but he had also been none too intelligent. When he had helped himself to the milk, he had left a clear set of fingerprints. The police had no problem in identifying them as those of petty criminal Eric Hobday. They now knew the identity of the man who had broken into the house in Bromford Lane, whom they strongly suspected as being the same man who had stabbed Charles Fox in Moor Street. All they had to do was to find him.

The police approached the BBC and asked them to broadcast a description of the wanted man. This had never been done before, and Eric Hobday made history by being the first man to have his description given out over the radio. The radio broadcast added that he was 'wanted in connection with a murder'.

Eric Hobday was heading north in a car – a Jowett, said to be worth over £100 – which he had stolen in West Bromwich, but while driving through Cheshire he somehow managed to roll the vehicle over. He abandoned the Jowett, leaving his suitcase inside, and set off on foot. The Cheshire police soon found the car and took possession of the suitcase. Although Hobday had been careful not to leave his fingerprints in the stolen car, he had forgotten about those on the vehicle's starting handle.

Some weeks later, in northern Cumberland, a cowman called Walter Barber was driving a herd of cattle to be milked when he spotted a diminutive stranger, and recognised him from the description given in the BBC broadcast he had heard earlier. But with a phlegmatic attitude that recalls that of Sir Francis Drake, Walter decided that getting the cows milked was more urgent than catching the murder suspect. It was two hours later that he told his employer, Mr J W Watt, about the stranger, and Mr Watt alerted the local police constable in nearby Mossband. PC Elder soon caught up with the fugitive, and Eric Hobday was arrested.

He was transported back to West Bromwich to be questioned. The police had the battered suitcase, and Hobday admitted that it was his. He claimed that he had left it in a field near West Bromwich earlier in the summer, explaining that he had been sleeping in a tent there until the farmer had moved him on. However, the police knew that the case had actually been discovered in the crashed Jowett, abandoned on a Cheshire road. Asked to describe the case's contents, Eric Hobday catalogued items of clothing, camping equipment and a sheath knife. Everything was there except the knife; that had been recovered from the body of Charles Fox, murdered by an intruder in his home in Moor Street.

Eric Hobday's trial took place in November 1933, before Mr Justice Talbot at Stafford Assizes, with Mr W G Earingey KC prosecuting. Chief Superintendent Cherrill gave evidence concerning the fingerprints found at the Bromford Lane break-in, and said that the knife's sheath had been discovered in the road between Moor Street and Bromford Lane. A rip in Hobday's jacket had been mended with cotton identical to that taken from Mr Newton's workbox. The stubble left on Mr Newton's razor matched that of Eric Hobday. A 14 year old boy who had seen Hobday when he was camping in the summer gave evidence that the accused man had owned a knife identical to the one used to kill Charles Fox.

Hobday's defence counsel, Sir Reginald Coventry KC, argued that it was inconceivable that anyone could stab a man to death, then break into another house, coolly shave himself and mend his clothes, then stop for a drink of milk.

However, the jury did find the sequence of events conceivable and, after a 35-minute deliberation, they found Eric Hobday guilty of murder. He was sentenced to death, and was hanged in Winson Green prison, Birmingham, in December 1933.

6

ABSENT
WITHOUT LEAVE

The Murder of Harry Berrisford in Birches Head, Hanley,
May 1946

Anyone hearing of a case of a body concealed under the floorboards of a house in Cromwell Street would immediately think of the 1995 case of Fred and Rosemary West in Gloucester. However, the case in question happened 49 years earlier, in the area of the Potteries known as Birches Head, near Hanley.

In 1946, Mrs Betty Berrisford and her 12 year old daughter Rachel were living at 6 Cromwell Street, Birches Head. Mrs Berrisford's 20 year old son Harry was a private in the army catering corps, but he always came home when he was on leave. Also living in the house, as lodgers, were 23 year old Irene Dunning and her common-law husband Stan Sheminant, a 28 year old driver.

The relationship between Irene and Stan had always been a tempestuous one. They had been about to marry until Irene broke off the engagement on discovering that her fiancé already had a wife and child. However, Stan had pleaded with her to resume their relationship and, in June 1945, she had taken him back to live with her in the house in Cromwell Street where she lodged. At first they shared an upstairs room, but soon moved downstairs to live in the front room.

Stan, a keen gambler, was always hard up and he made ends meet by selling or pawning items belonging to the Berrisfords. He sold the bed that he and Irene slept in, with the result that they had to sleep on a mattress on the floor. He stole Harry Berrisford's bicycle and sold it for £1, and from time to time he pawned Harry's suit to raise extra cash.

On Friday 17th May, Harry returned home from his camp in Lincoln. He visited his mother at Maddock & Sons, where she worked as a pottery caster, then set off for Cromwell Street. When he reached home he spoke to Stan and Irene, and Irene fried him a couple of eggs. As there was no coal in the house, Irene set off to pick some from the nearby coal tip, leaving Harry talking to Stan Sheminant.

When she returned with two bags of coal at 4.45 pm, she went into the kitchen. She could hear a lot of hammering coming from the downstairs front room, and Stan emerged to explain that he had been laying some lino. Irene asked where Harry was, only to be told that he had taken his kit bag, and departed. Stan warned Irene to tell Mrs Berrisford that she had seen Harry leave, as he did not want her to know that he had not been to work that day. When Irene asked why the hammer she used for breaking coal was lying on the kitchen table, Stan simply told her to return it to its usual place.

When Mrs Berrisford came home, she asked where Harry was. Irene did as she had been told, saying that Harry had said 'Cheerio' to her before leaving. Over supper, Mrs Berrisford asked Stan if he had seen Harry that day. Stan Sheminant coolly stated that Harry had already left the house before he got home from work.

That night, as Irene and Stan went to bed on the mattress on the front-room floor, Irene was still puzzled about Harry Berrisford's disappearance. She said as much, and Stan replied that he had 'done away with him'. He pointed to the floor beneath the mattress, and said, 'He's in there.' Irene was disgusted at Stan's warped sense of humour and told him not to talk soft. The next morning, Stan Sheminant said to her that what he had told her was true, adding that she had better not say anything about it or she would be 'in it as much as he was.' When Irene attempted to leave the house, saying she did not want to stay with him any longer, Sheminant again threatened her, then gave her a beating to emphasise his warning.

When the missing soldier failed to return to his army camp in Lincoln, he was deemed absent without leave, a potential deserter. Members of the military police called several times at the house in Cromwell Street, trying to discover his whereabouts. However, Private Harry Berrisford had disappeared without trace.

On 21st May, Stan Sheminant moved his mattress back upstairs, and he and Irene Dunning began to sleep in the front bedroom. The room below was now kept locked and Stan looked after the key himself, allowing no one else to enter. From time to time, Irene heard hammering coming from the locked room, but Sheminant continued to warn her to keep her mouth shut.

Towards the end of May, Stan was again short of money, but Irene refused to borrow any more from her relatives. In the end, the couple went to Hanley, where Stan forced Irene to borrow £10 using Mrs Berrisford's name. In June, Mrs Berrisford noticed that Stan was wearing her missing son's trousers. She was furious, and Stan did apologise to her. It was about this time that Stan suggested that they could advertise in the *News of the World* to try to trace Harry.

By now, Mrs Berrisford was desperately anxious about her son, and when the family dog, Crackers, developed a habit of scratching at the locked front-room door, she decided to take action. On Monday 8th July, at 5 am, she used a kitchen knife to force open the Yale lock. Once inside, she removed the linoleum from the floor, and discovered that a piece of the floor boarding was loose. She felt under the board and touched what might have been a human leg covered in cloth. Terrified, she left the room, slamming the door shut. Immediately, Sheminant came running downstairs, and Mrs Berrisford left the house and went off to work.

For once, Stan Sheminant was in work that day, but when he came home, he insisted that Irene go to meet Mrs Berrisford from Maddock & Sons and take her to the pictures. He even gave her the money to pay for the seats! The next day, Mrs Berrisford spoke to a police officer in Birches Head, and as a result, police officers went to 6 Cromwell Street. They made a search but found nothing.

Eleven days later, Mrs Berrisford again went into the front room, accompanied by her two sisters and Irene Dunning. Together they lifted the lino. The floorboards seemed to have been freshly nailed down, but they managed to prise up a shorter, offcut board. Underneath there appeared to be soil, but Mrs Berrisford thought she could feel a piece of cloth. Again, she went to fetch the police. This time two constables came back with her, and lifted several floorboards. When they shifted some of the earth beneath, they uncovered a decaying body.

At 4.45 pm, Detective Superintendent Edwin Till arrived at the house with Professor James Webster, a Home Office pathologist. The body was in a shallow grave directly under the floorboards, soil having been scooped out sufficiently to allow the corpse to lie under the joists. The dead man was dressed in khaki trousers and shirt, but was barefoot. Once the body had been lifted out, other items were found underneath it. These included an army battledress and beret, a towel, shaving brush and toothbrush. There was also a haversack bearing Private Harry Berrisford's regimental number. The whereabouts of the young soldier, once suspected of being a deserter, were no longer a mystery.

The post-mortem on Harry's body, conducted by Professor Webster, established that death had occurred some 8 to 12 weeks earlier and had been caused by repeated blows to the head with a blunt instrument, resulting in skull fractures and intracranial haemorrhage.

After the police had spoken to Mrs Berrisford and Irene Dunning, they arrested Stan Sheminant. On Saturday 20th July, he appeared before stipendiary magistrate Mr R N Macgregor Clarkson at a special court in Hanley, charged with the wilful murder of Harry Berrisford on or about 17th May. He was remanded in custody.

On 20th November, the trial of Stanley Sheminant began at the Stafford Assizes before Mr Justice Hilbery. In his opening statement, Mr W H Cartwright Sharp KC, the prosecuting counsel, said that the accused and the dead youth were alone together from about 2.45 pm until 4.45 pm on Friday 17th May. The evidence would indicate that at some point during those two hours, the accused hit the young man a blow on the back of the head which sent him to the floor, and then struck repeated blows with a heavy instrument such as a hammer, shattering the skull on both sides of the head. Sheminant then proceeded to take up some floorboards near the hearth in the downstairs front room. He carved out a section of a joist to make room for the body, then pushed the dead man into a shallow grave. After nailing the floorboards down, he put some linoleum down on top of them.

Professor James Webster gave evidence that the blows to the dead soldier's head could not have been self-inflicted. He had also concluded that the dead man had not struck any blows in self-defence, nor warded off any blows. He told the court that a cloth belt had been tightly tied around the neck, but in his opinion this had been done after death. A piece of sacking had been placed over the dead man's head.

Stanley Sheminant, called by the defence to give evidence in his own defence, told the court that he and Harry Berrisford were friends, and usually on the best of terms. He claimed that on the afternoon of 17th May, he had been laying some lino in the front room, when Harry Berrisford came into the house. They greeted each other in a friendly way, then Irene Dunning went into the kitchen to cook Harry something to eat.

After Irene had left the house, Sheminant went into the kitchen to get some tacks, and Harry Berrisford had asked him what had happened to his suit. Sheminant admitted that he had pawned it while he was out of work, and Harry had called him a thief. Harry had become very angry, making derogatory comments about Irene Dunning's morals, and Stanley Sheminant had answered with similar comments about Mrs Berrisford. Sheminant told the court that Harry Berrisford had seized a pan of boiling water, and in fear that it was going to be thrown at him, he had punched the young soldier in the face. Harry had fallen backwards to the floor, and pulled Stan down with him. The two angry men had grappled on the floor, and Sheminant admitted seizing Harry's head and 'banging it'. When he recovered from his daze, he saw a pool of blood underneath Harry's head and on the hearthstone. The youth was dead. In a state of fear and panic he had attempted to conceal the body by burying it under the floor.

In his summing-up, Mr Justice Hilbery told the jury that if they accepted Stanley Sheminant's account, they might consider a manslaughter verdict. However, he reminded them that after concealing the body under the floor, the accused had slept on a mattress on the very spot, making love to his 'paramour' only inches above the rotting corpse. He must have been very conscious of that fact, and it was not surprising, therefore, that he had confessed as much to Miss Dunning. The judge also contrasted the fear and panic described by the accused with the very practical way in which he had carried on with his life after the death of Harry Berrisford.

The all-male jury retired for only half an hour before returning a verdict of guilty. The judge said that he agreed with their verdict and sentenced Stanley Sheminant to death. An appeal to the Lord Chief Justice failed, and Sheminant was hanged at Walton Prison, Liverpool, on 3rd January 1947.

7

THE
APPROVED SCHOOL BREAK-OUT

The Murder of William Peter Fieldhouse at Standon Farm
Approved School, near Eccleshall
February 1947

T he winter of 1946–7 was particularly severe, one of the coldest on record. Frozen snow covered the entire country for months. Even in the relative warmth of private homes, people were finding it hard to live their normal lives. At Standon Farm Approved School, near Eccleshall, things were even worse. The school, owned by the Children's Society, had been built in 1885 as a home for waifs and strays, but in 1938 it had become an approved school for boys aged between 13 and 16. All of the 65 young residents were fed up with the conditions there, and some of the older boys began to talk about making a break-out. It was in February of 1947 that a group of 15–16 year old inmates devised a desperate and brutal plan to murder the headmaster, Thomas Dawson, to steal his car, and to make their escape in it. One reason behind the plot was that Mr Dawson regarded 12 months as insufficient time for an inmate to get any benefit from the school, and so would not issue a licence for any boy to return home after only one year. The boys also resented Mr Dawson's withholding of pocket money as a punishment.

One of the boys, a non-commissioned officer in the army cadet unit of the 2nd North Staffs based at the school, was a natural-born leader. By a mixture of threats, bribes and personal charisma, he organised other youngsters into stealing the food and clothing that would be needed during the journey. Initially the escape was timed to take place during the monthly staff meeting. The duty master was to be locked in the boiler room, then the boys would burst into the staff meeting with guns and kill Mr Dawson. However, they became impatient and

LOCKER ROOM: Mr. Fieldhouse found shot here

Standon Farm Approved School. (Staffordshire Police Museum)

decided that they could not wait until the day of the meeting, and it was therefore on Saturday 15th February that the final parts of the conspiracy were put into effect. One group of boys forced the door into the cadet corps armoury and stole three Lee Enfield service rifles, while a second group broke into the headmaster's private house to obtain the ammunition.

At 1.30 in the afternoon, four boys were in the bathroom, loading bullets into the rifles, when the door opened. There stood 21 year old Peter Fieldhouse, the assistant gardening master at the school, who had been left in sole charge of the 65 boys during the lunch break. When Peter Fieldhouse demanded to know what they thought they were doing, one boy fired a rifle at him, but missed. He fired a second shot and this hit Mr Fieldhouse in the groin, bringing him down. As he lay helpless on the floor, the boy reloaded the gun and deliberately fired a third shot into his chest.

These desperately improvised events were caused by panic and were definitely not part of the carefully devised plan. Abandoning their original intentions of killing the headmaster and stealing his car, the boys dropped their weapons and made their getaway on foot. The ten escapees made their way across country, fighting through heavy snowdrifts, to Stableford, where they managed to get onto the LMS railway line and headed towards Madeley. It was easier going along the track, but the boys were spotted by a railway signalman.

Back at the school, one young inmate who had heard the shots rushed to fetch the headmaster. Thomas Dawson took one look at the injured master, then immediately sent for the police and a doctor. However, the medical attention came too late: Peter Fieldhouse had been fatally wounded and he died just before 2 o'clock, half an hour

PC Luther Sumnall. (Staffordshire Police Museum)

after the shooting. A massive police hunt for his killers was put into effect, with police cars searching the snow-covered lanes and roads in the area.

At about 5.30 that afternoon two police constables – PC Sumnall and PC Holleran – caught nine of the boys on the railway line between Madeley and Crewe. The boys were easily arrested, but Luther Sumnall, a former drill corporal with the Lancashire Regiment, had to pursue a tenth boy across fields. He caught him after a 20-minute chase, when the fugitive was slowed down in a deep snowdrift.

The ten boys were taken to Newcastle-under-Lyme police station, where they were questioned by Detective Superintendent Tom Lockley. As the boys were initially unwilling to say which of them had shot at Peter Fieldhouse, Tom Lockley made the highly unusual decision to charge all ten with the murder. After being charged, the ten youngsters conferred among themselves and elected a spokesman, who made a statement: 'I will speak for the lot and tell the truth. We made it up last Tuesday. We got fed up with school and we planned to shoot the headmaster. There were ten of us. We were going to pinch the headmaster's car and some stores and get away. Two of us can drive. We planned it for the next staff meeting but it was too long to wait.'

Back at the school, all privileges were stopped for the remaining 55 inmates. No visitors were allowed, and the next day's morning church parade and afternoon walk were both cancelled. The choir master at All Saints' church in Standon village was Bill Fieldhouse, Peter's father, so it is perhaps not surprising that those Standon Farm boys who were also members of the church choir were not allowed to attend the evening service. At that service, the rector, the Rev C W Salt, asked the members of his congregation to pray for the dead man, his parents, and his sister.

The trial of the ten accused boys was held at Stafford Assizes less than a month after the killing. Under examination, the headmaster, Thomas Dawson, stated that eight of the ten boys were mentally subnormal. PC Luther Sumnall described how he had arrested nine of the boys on the Madeley-Crewe railway line, and the tenth approximately 20 minutes later.

A statement made later by this boy was read to the court: 'Between 1.30 and 2 pm today, I was in the bathroom at Standon Farm School with three rifles when Mr Peter Fieldhouse walked through the door and asked what I was doing. I pulled the trigger and shot him. That shot missed. I pulled the trigger again and that shot hit him and he fell to the ground. I reloaded and shot at him again. Then we all made a run for it.'

The jury took only 30 minutes to arrive at their verdicts. Four of the boys were found guilty of murdering Mr Fieldhouse and were sentenced to be detained during His Majesty's pleasure. Two others were sent to Borstal and three others received varying sentences for conspiracy to murder. The tenth boy was acquitted.

After the trial, the Chief Constable of Staffordshire, Colonel Sir Herbert Hunter, stated: 'I have to specially place on record my strong appreciation of the very excellent team work, intelligence and tenacity under difficult conditions of all ranks concerned with the recent round-up and capture of the criminals in the murder case. Rarely have I seen a case showing such a record of swift and able investigation, co-operation and good understanding.' PC Holleran and PC Sumnall each received a commendation.

Following an inquiry into the running of Standon Farm Approved School, a report was issued criticising the facilities, the discipline and the day-to-day running of the institution. Mr Dawson was dismissed and the school was closed down.

One person who feels that these decisions were wrong is Frederick Brashay, himself an inmate at the school from July 1942 until January 1945. Fred, who was born in Ripon workhouse and had spent some unhappy years in various institutions, says that going to Standon Farm School was the best thing that ever happened to him. He remembers Mr and Mrs Dawson – the headmaster's wife was the matron of the school – as caring and encouraging. In his autobiography, *Going Back*, Fred quotes many examples of their support and generosity, remembering that they bought him a full set of tools when he left the school to take up a joinery apprenticeship at the Lotus Shoe Company in Stafford. The facilities at Standon Farm School were better than at most schools, Fred states, and in this case the headmaster was used as a scapegoat.

8

THE
STERN GANG KILLING

The Murder of Rex Farran at Codsall
May 1948

Captain Roy Farran, the eldest of four brothers, was a soldier whose wartime exploits in the Special Air Service were both clandestine and heroic. Initially serving with the King's Own Hussars, he joined the SAS at its formation in 1943 and served in Tunisia, Sicily, Greece, Italy and France, frequently operating behind enemy lines. In 1945, he and a small group of men parachuted into Italy to work with the Italian partisans in the Apennine mountains. One of Roy Farran's audacious feats was to lead a successful attack on the German Corps headquarters at Albinea. Roy's wartime heroism was recognised by the award of the French Croix de Guerre, the American Legion of Merit, and in Britain by the Military Cross and two bars, and the Distinguished Service Order.

After the war, Roy Farran stood in the 1945 general election as the Conservative candidate for the Black Country constituency of Dudley and Stourbridge, but he was not elected. He also wrote an auto-biographical account of his wartime exploits in the SAS. This book, entitled *Winged Dagger: Adventures on Special Service*, was accepted for publication by Collins and was scheduled to be published in 1948.

Later, he became an undercover agent in Palestine, organising the special-duties Q Squads which were formed to investigate and sabotage the activities of the Stern Gang. This organisation was founded in 1940 by Avraham Stern, following a split in the under-ground Irgun movement. The Stern Gang, or *Lehi*, were either violent terrorists or determined fighters for the freedom of Israel, depending on who is writing the history. They were fanatically anti-British during World War II and, in contrast to the firmly anti-Nazi Irgun movement, even invited help from the Axis powers to drive the British out of Palestine.

Although Stern himself was killed by the police in February 1942, his organisation continued its terrorist activities after his death. In November 1944, the Stern Gang assassinated Lord Moyne, a British Minister of State. Irgun too was still active in violent anti-British activity, and in 1946 its members blew up the headquarters of the British administration in Palestine, the King David Hotel in Jerusalem. This atrocity killed 88 people, including Britons, Arabs and Jews. When the authorities began to flog and to hang captured terrorists, Irgun and the Stern Gang developed a strategy of kidnapping British hostages and retaliating in kind. Although most Jews sympathised with the aim of establishing an independent state of Israel after the end of the war, the vast majority disapproved of the terrorists' use of bombs and bullets to achieve this aim.

Roy Farran's Q Squads were formed to fight the terrorist groups at their own game and with their own tactics. When a 15 year old member of the Stern Gang, Alexander Rubowitz, disappeared after being abducted by a Q Squad on 6th May 1947, there was a public outcry. In October, Captain Roy Farran was tried by a general court martial in Jerusalem, on the charge of murdering the missing boy.

Evidence was given that on 6th May, Alexander Rubowitz had been distributing Stern Gang literature when he was intercepted by members of a Q Squad. Witnesses said that he had been chased by a man, who caught him, bundled him into a saloon car containing two other men, and drove off. The boy had not been seen since, and his parents had been notified that he was 'presumably dead'. During the chase, the man who had caught the youth had lost his hat, which was found later at the scene. This hat was produced in court, and had the letters FAR–AN (with the fourth letter missing) written inside it. A witness also identified Capt Farran as the man who had abducted the missing youth.

Much legal debate took place when Roy Farran's defence counsel objected to the admissibility as evidence of documents written by Captain Farran while in custody, arguing that these were notes prepared by the accused officer for his defence; they were therefore privileged and could not be used against him. When the court martial ruled in favour of this argument, the defence then argued that as Rubowitz's body had not been found, there was no case to answer. The court martial concurred and acquitted Roy Farran.

However, the Stern Gang never accepted the court martial verdict

A window at The Myron, Histons Hill, Codsall. (*Express & Star*)

and swore revenge. Graffiti appeared on walls in Tel Aviv and other towns, and leaflets were distributed stating that Captain Farran's time would come, and promising that he would be pursued to the ends of the earth. Capt Farran left Palestine and returned to live at the family home in Codsall, Staffordshire.

At 8 o'clock on the morning of Monday 3rd May 1948, postwoman Eileen Hayes delivered a parcel to The Myron, a house on Histons Hill, Codsall. It was addressed to Captain Roy Farran, but he was away in Scotland, accompanied by a police bodyguard. Eileen Hayes actually handed the parcel over to Roy's 26 year old brother, Rex.

As Eileen went back down the drive, Rex Farran took the parcel into the house. A special brick safety-chamber had been installed in the house into which suspicious objects could be placed, but Rex had no occasion to suspect that anything was amiss. He could tell that the package contained a book, and immediately thought it must be a copy of *Winged Dagger*. Rex was keen to see a copy of his brother's work, and decided to open the parcel himself.

As he opened the parcel, it exploded. The whole house shook and Rex Farran received horrendous injuries to his legs and abdomen. He was rushed four miles to the Wolverhampton Royal Hospital for emergency treatment, but died two hours later. His death was later recorded as due to haemorrhage and shock.

Subsequent forensic investigation of the pieces of the parcel proved that it had indeed contained a book. It was not *Winged Dagger* as Rex had assumed, but a copy of the complete plays of William Shakespeare. The book had been hollowed out, and inside it there had been a fragment bomb attached to a battery. The whole thing was a boobytrap device, designed to explode when the parcel was opened.

Police inquiries revealed that the particular edition of Shakespeare plays had been available at many metropolitan and provincial bookshops, and they were unable to find where it had been purchased. The postmark on what remained of the parcel's wrappings showed that it had been posted in the East End of London. Roy Farran informed the police that he had received threatening letters, also posted in east London, the previous October. They had contained a single piece of paper bearing one word – Revenge – written in Hebrew. Scotland Yard detectives began an immediate investigation of all known Stern Gang sympathisers living in London. They also checked recent immigration records against a list of Stern Gang members, and asked other European police forces to do the same.

The Boulton & Paul football team in April 1948, three days before the death of Rex Farran, who is on the far right, back row. (Mrs N Hill)

Although the police could find no direct evidence linking the Stern Gang with the killing, a British news agency in Paris received a telephone call the day after the murder. The caller claimed to be a Stern Gang spokesman and said that the killing had been their response to the British government's decision to send further troops to Palestine, as well as a personal revenge for the death of Alexander Rubowitz.

If the call was genuine – and it was widely accepted that it was – then the personal revenge aimed at Roy Farran killed the wrong man, a young engineering draughtsman who had absolutely no connection with the politics of the Middle East. Vince Cresswell, who played in the same works football team as the murdered man, recalls that whether the team won or lost, Rex never complained or bragged about the result. Joan Cooper was a friend of the Farran family, and she too remembers Rex as a cheerful and likeable young man. Joan's husband and Rex Farran were both employed at the Boulton & Paul aircraft factory in Wolverhampton, and they were all together at the firm's social club the night before the killing. It was a warm evening, and they were sitting outside having a drink. Joan recalls Rex Farran sitting her one year old son on his knee and playing with him. 'He was a

Captain Roy Farran kneels at his brother's grave. (*Express & Star*)

wonderful young man,' she told me, 'always smiling. We just could not believe it when he was killed by the letter bomb the next day. What sort of people could do that to someone like Rex?'

Rex Farran's funeral was held in Codsall on Friday 7th May, and was attended by his parents and brothers, his former colleagues from Boulton & Paul, his soccer team-mates, and his many friends. Together they mourned the loss of a young man who, in the words of Vince Cresswell, 'never made an enemy in his life'.

Roy Farran, who had to live with the memory that his younger brother had been blown up by a bomb intended for him, later emigrated to Canada, where he eventually became a newspaper proprietor in Calgary.

9

DEATH
OF A HEADMISTRESS

The Murder of Miss Winifred Mulley at Burton upon Trent
July 1951

In 1951, Miss Winifred Mulley, the 52 year old headmistress of Burton Girls' High School, lived alone in a house called The Woodlands, situated in the grounds of the school. There were no other residential houses nearby. The High School had broken up for the summer holidays on Wednesday 25th July, and Miss Mulley had been due to go away on holiday on the following Monday morning. She had booked a taxi to take her to the railway station, but then cancelled it, deciding to travel after the holiday rush. Miss Mulley had recently completed the purchase of a house in Stapenhill, and had been intending to move in after her holiday.

On the morning of Tuesday 31st July, Mrs Emily Plummer, who had been Miss Mulley's daily help for three and a half years, went to The Woodlands at 9.45 am. There was no sign of Miss Mulley, so Mrs Plummer went upstairs to the landing and knocked on her bedroom door. There was no reply, so she tried the door and found it was locked. Mrs Plummer went downstairs to begin her chores, but, worried by the very unusual occurrence of the locked bedroom door, she went up and knocked again a quarter of an hour later. There was still no reply, and she resumed her domestic work.

Later, when she went to make herself a cup of tea, the daily noticed that the teapot had been used and that there was a dirty cup and saucer on the table. Mrs Plummer washed them up. Oddly, the tea caddy was not in its usual place and had been left with its lid off.

She returned to the locked bedroom door four times during the morning, and at 12 o'clock she peered through the keyhole. There was no key in the lock, so Mrs Plummer got a key from another bedroom

61

The Woodlands, where Miss Mulley was murdered. (*Burton Mail*)

door and tried it. It fitted, so she unlocked the door and went in, calling out to her employer. She noticed that there was blood on the bed and that the eiderdown was pulled right to the top, completely covering Miss Mulley.

Realising that something was drastically wrong, Mrs Plummer hurried downstairs to summon help. She met George Chatterton, the school's head gardener, who came back to the bedroom with her. He pulled down the eiderdown to find that Miss Mulley was dead, with a small penknife protruding from her neck. George pulled the eiderdown back over the dead woman's face, and sent for the police. The first policeman on the scene was PC Chidlow, who took one look at the body before notifying his senior officers.

Miss Mulley's pyjama-clad body had severe head injuries, as well as the stab wound caused by the penknife. On the bedside table were two unopened tins, one of anchovies and the other of sausages. Initially, some attention was given to a crushed sprig of deadly nightshade found on the bedroom carpet, but it was stated later that this was of no significance and could have been brought in on the shoe of someone entering the room after the time of death. The pearl-handled penknife used to stab Miss Mulley was believed to have been her own property, and to have been normally kept on her bedside table.

Chief Superintendent Tom Lockley, head of Staffordshire CID, arrived and immediately sought the advice of Professor J M Webster, a Home Office pathologist based at the West Midlands forensic science laboratory. Professor Webster arrived at 4 pm and made his initial examination at The Woodlands. He noted that the right foot was twisted up behind the body in an awkward and unnatural position. Miss Mulley had sustained injuries to her head and neck and had two black eyes, an area of superficial damage to the forehead, and a single cut on the hairline. There were also abrasions to the jaw.

The body was then taken to the borough mortuary for a more detailed autopsy. It was found that the bruises had been caused by a blunt instrument, and the cuts by a different sharp instrument. The injuries were not self-inflicted and were likely to have been caused by a woman or a small man. These findings led police to instigate a murder hunt, and to call in the help of Scotland Yard officers.

Emily Plummer was able to tell the police that she had last seen her employer on the afternoon of the previous day, Monday, when the two of them had chatted for about 20 minutes before Mrs Plummer left The Woodlands at 2.30 pm. Miss Mulley had at that time been alive and well.

George Chatterton recalled that when he arrived at work on the Monday morning, he had found a young man sleeping rough in one of the greenhouses. When asked what he was doing there, the man had replied that he had missed his last bus to Derby and did not fancy the 10-mile walk home, so he had spent the night sleeping in the school grounds. George Chatterton had asked him which part of Derby he came from, and had been told Kedleston Road. The youth had then left the premises.

The police were able to establish that the young man had left Burton that morning. He had been seen near Repton at 10.15 am by a schoolboy, Dennis Poxon. At 4 pm the same day, he was seen again in the village of Newton Solney, apparently heading back towards Burton.

On 1st August, the police issued a statement to the press, saying that they were anxious to trace a youth who had been seen in the vicinity over the weekend. They described him as: 'Aged about 16 to 17, medium height, slim build, slim hips, light brown hair, wearing a fairly good blue pinstripe suit, brown shoes, which were badly in need of cleaning, rather unkempt appearance.'

A man of similar description was seen at Burton railway station in the early hours of Tuesday morning, about 12 hours before Miss Mulley's body was found. He used two pound notes to purchase a single ticket to Bristol, catching the 12.40 am train. Three porters who observed him standing, hands in pockets, on the platform described him as thin and pasty-faced, with rough hair. Later, detectives went to the Burton branch of Lloyds Bank and examined a number of pound notes paid in from Burton station. One of them – number C58B 336068 – was found to have blood smears on it.

On Tuesday 7th August, the police announced that they were looking for a 20 year old army deserter named John Fenton, who they thought could help them with their investigations into the murder of Winifred Mulley. Fenton had been missing from his Royal Pioneer Corps camp in Lockerbie, Dumfriesshire, since 27th July. His home address was given as Kedleston Road, Derby. He was described as being 20 years old, 5 ft 7 in tall, slim with a pale complexion.

At 5 am on 9th August, Tom Lockley, head of Staffordshire CID, and Superintendent John Black of Scotland Yard were on their way to Worthing, where the man they wished to interview had been arrested by the Sussex police. Private John Fenton had been found sleeping under a boat on Worthing beach. At Brighton police station, Fenton was questioned by the two detectives and, after being cautioned, he dictated a statement to them. By 10.30 am, Fenton and the two detectives were on their way back to Burton police station, where they arrived at 3 pm.

John Fenton was charged with the murder of Winifred Mulley and appeared at Burton magistrates' court on 10th and 17th August, each time being remanded in custody. His full committal trial began on 24th August. Mr William Lewis, prosecuting, read from Fenton's statement, in which the soldier said that he had deserted from the army because he was afraid of retaliation from a fellow soldier whom he had reported for stealing. On the first night, a Saturday, he had gone to a cinema in Carlisle, then slept in a field. The next day, he had walked to Penrith where he slept in a wood. He then used most of his money – he only had 10 shillings with him – on the bus fare to Kendal, where he slept in an empty lorry. When the driver returned, Fenton hid in the lorry and was transported to Burton. At about 4.30 pm, he wandered into the grounds of an empty school and ate some apples from a tree. He slept in a greenhouse, and was spoken to by the gardener the next morning, then walked to Repton and back.

He re-entered the grounds of Burton Girls' High School, intending to spend another night in the greenhouse. He saw the house next to the school, and hid in the bushes, watching. When he saw no one around, he assumed that the house was empty. He entered through the kitchen window, and began to look for food. He ate a piece of bread and jam, then stole two tins from the pantry, along with a tin-opener which he had found on the draining board. He ventured upstairs and had almost reached the bathroom, when he heard a noise. A woman in pyjamas came out of a bedroom and grabbed him by the arm, saying, 'What do you think you are doing?'

Fenton said that he must have lost his head, and he began hitting the woman with the bigger of the two tins he had taken from the pantry. 'We struggled into the bedroom until we reached the bed. I hit her again with the tin and she seemed unconscious. I then saw the knife on the bedside table. It was an ordinary penknife. My mind was in such a mess I didn't know what I was doing, and stabbed it in her neck.'

When he realised what he had done, he thought about committing suicide, but decided he had better get away. After covering his victim with the eiderdown, the young soldier spotted Miss Mulley's handbag on the table, and took £5 from it. There was a key in the bedroom door, so he locked the door and took the key with him. He went straight to Burton station and bought a ticket to Bristol, paying with money he had taken from Miss Mulley's bag. There was some time to wait, so he went into Burton and bought some chips. He threw away the key to the bedroom door, returned to the station and slept in the waiting room until the train was due.

He got to Bristol at 5.30 am and caught the next train to Taunton. After spending a day there, he took a train to Brighton, where he spent the rest of his money. Since then, he had been sleeping in a dinghy on Worthing beach, 'hoping I would die of something'.

The prosecution told the court that the owner of the boat saw Fenton and fetched a policeman. At first Fenton claimed to be staying in Brighton with his mother, but when PC Lacey found a diary in his pocket indicating that he was a serving soldier, he admitted that he was a deserter. He was taken to Brighton police station for further questioning.

The prosecution counsel told the court that a bloodstained jacket found on the train in which John Fenton travelled from Burton to Bristol had been taken to the West Midlands forensic science laboratory for examination. Biological assistant John Merchant gave evidence that he had compared woollen fibres taken from beneath the fingernails of the murdered woman with fibres from the blue jacket and found them 'microscopically indistinguishable'.

Professor Webster gave evidence of the findings from his post-mortem autopsy. He said that Miss Mulley received two types of injury to her face and head, inflicted with a blunt instrument and with a cutting instrument. She also had cuts on her hands which indicated that she had not died without a struggle. The knife in her neck had not hit any main vessels and this wound had not bled; the considerable amount of blood found on her bed had come from her head injuries. Professor Webster had come to the conclusion that the stab wound was one of her last injuries, and that she had lived for some time after the injuries had been inflicted. He was handed the tin of sausages found at the murder scene and confirmed to the court that it could have caused some of the blunter injuries to the body.

Chief Superintendent Tom Lockley gave evidence concerning the questioning of John Fenton at Brighton police station, saying that he had been present when Fenton's statement was made.

After a six-hour hearing, John Fenton was committed for trial at the next Stafford Assizes. He appeared before Mr Justice Streatfeild on 28th November. Prosecuting counsel, E Sachs KC, told the jury that in many ways the case was not unique. A young soldier – of not particularly high intelligence – went absent without leave, slept rough, got hungry, and was short of cash. Fenton had got into a house to find food and to steal, and was surprised by Miss Mulley. He attacked her with one of the tins from his pocket. Whether it was from fright, from a determination to escape, or from temper, did not in the end matter very much.

Obviously anticipating a possible line that the defence might pursue, Mr Sachs proceeded to outline matters of law to the jury, explaining that the physical definition of murder was killing with malice aforethought. However, he wanted them to know that the phrase *malice aforethought* did not necessarily imply what might be called a 'planned murder'. Any act by a person in the course of committing a felony, if that act was one of violence and resulted in death, was murder. He also stressed that there was no such defence as sudden impulse. Insanity was a very different thing from uncontrollable impulse, and was not constituted by low intelligence, or by a man being a poor type, or miserable. A man was only insane, in the eyes of the law, if he did not know the physical nature and quality of the act, or did not know it was wrong.

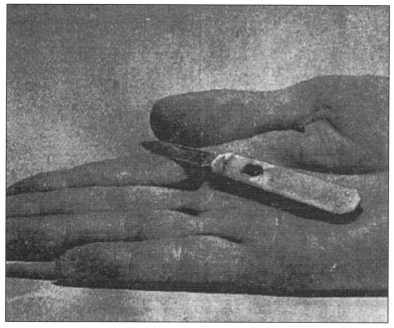

The knife with which Miss Mulley was stabbed. (*Burton Mail*)

The prosecution took the jury through all that John Fenton had done between running away from camp on 27th July and his arrest in Worthing on 8th August. Mr Sachs drew the attention of the jury to two phrases in John Fenton's statement. In the first Fenton had said that he must have 'lost his head' when he took out the tin and began to hit Miss Mulley with it. One interpretation of this was that Fenton had lost his head through fright. In the other phrase Fenton had claimed that his mind was in 'such a mess' that he did not know what he was doing when he picked up the knife and stabbed Miss Mulley in the neck. Mr Sachs suggested that Fenton had indeed known what he was doing: he saw the knife, picked it up and stuck it in Miss Mulley's neck.

Witnesses, including Emily Plummer, PC Chidlow and Professor Webster, gave evidence of the events of 30th and 31st July, repeating what they had told the earlier magistrates' court. Detective Superintendent Livings of the fingerprint division of Scotland Yard told the jury that prints taken from the tin of sausages and other articles in Miss Mulley's house tallied with those taken from John Fenton after his arrest.

Fenton's defence was led by Mr A J Long, the Recorder of Wolverhampton. He called Dr Lescher, physician to the Derby Royal Infirmary, who told the court that he had examined John Fenton on 15th and 21st August and had studied his history. He said that Fenton's father had committed suicide when John was 18 months old, and that John had suffered from meningitis as a child. He explained that meningitis was an inflammation of the brain lining, and sometimes affected the brain cells. One of the results of his father's death was that John Fenton had been a mother's boy from early times. He had never had a girlfriend. He found it hard to hold down a job, and had twice given up work to go home to his mother, whom he regarded as his only friend. His dirty personal habits were another sign of his low mental ability. When he was in the army, some of his clothes went missing and he reported their theft. Then he began to worry about what terrible things the thief might do to him when he came back from leave and found that Fenton had informed on him. When he broke into the house in Burton he had been without food for three days and his blood-sugar level would have been low. Tests had indicated that Fenton had abnormal reactions to low sugar levels. Dr Lescher said that he had come to the conclusion that Fenton was a grossly feeble-minded person whose brain cells were not working properly.

Cross-examined by the prosecution, Dr Lescher said that he could not name any disease Fenton was suffering, but he was of such low intelligence that he could be regarded as a child. When asked whether Fenton would have known what he was doing when he struck Miss Mulley with the tin, Dr Lescher said that, in his opinion, he would. Asked whether Fenton would know that what he was doing was wrong, the witness said that there were certain factors that might have affected his reasoning.

Mr Justice Streatfeild intervened, and asked Dr Lescher, 'Does it amount to this: that you believe he did know what he was doing, that he did know it was wrong, qualified only by reason of the abnormally low intelligence, his childishness, and the other factors you have enumerated which made him less capable of controlling himself?' The doctor concurred.

In his final speech, the defence counsel conceded that Fenton knew that what he was doing was wrong, but argued that he only knew it in a qualified sense, as a child would understand it.

Replying for the Crown, Mr Sachs said that the jury had to administer not sympathy, but justice according to the law. He urged them not to forget Miss Mulley, who was brutally murdered. He said that the unlucky young man was a social misfit, and that was a misfortune. He went on to say that it was equally a misfortune for Miss Mulley to be murdered by a misfit. Mr Sachs analysed Fenton's confession in detail and asked the jury to conclude that it was not the statement of a man who did not know what he was doing.

In his summing-up, the judge paid tribute to the gallantry of Miss Mulley, shown in the stout defence she put up. He remarked on the sad irony that, had she gone away on holiday as planned, she would have still been alive. He said that the jury might conclude that the accused had both the appearance and the mentality of a boy. However, it was his duty to tell them that there was no evidence that could possibly justify a verdict of manslaughter.

The jury retired for 58 minutes. When they returned, the clerk of the assize asked whether they found the prisoner guilty, or guilty while insane. The foreman replied, 'guilty, with a strong recommendation to mercy owing to mental immaturity.' Fenton received the verdict without any display of emotion, and stood rigid as the black cap was placed on Mr Justice Streatfeild's head, and the death sentence was imposed. The judge told Fenton, 'The jury have found you guilty of wilful murder, a verdict which in my opinion was the only one possible on this evidence. The recommendation to mercy will be forwarded by me to the proper quarter.'

On the application of the defence counsel, the judge directed that Fenton's mother, who had remained outside the court while the sentence was pronounced, could see her son. Fenton showed no emotion as he went down the steps to the cells. In December, the Home Secretary acted on the jury's recommendation and the death sentence was commuted to life imprisonment.

10

THE
ALIBI

The Murder of Mrs Alice Wiltshaw at Barlaston
July 1952

Frederick Wiltshaw was in the daily habit of stopping off for a hand of bridge at Trentham Golf Club on the way home from his pottery factory – Wiltshaw and Robinson Ltd – in Stoke-on-Trent. On the afternoon of Wednesday 16th July 1952, Frederick left the pottery at 4.15 pm, enjoyed his usual game at the Trentham club until just after 6 o'clock, then drove home to the village of Barlaston. He pulled into the drive of Estoril, his 14-room detached house, and put the car into the garage round the back. As he entered the kitchen he saw a chaotic scene: there was blood on the tablecloth and the walls. On the floor there was a saucepan and spilled vegetables. Nearby were two large logs both covered with blood.

Thinking that his wife had met with some terrible domestic accident, Frederick hurried into the hall. There, to his horror, he saw Alice lying dead on the hall floor, her face battered and unrecognisable. Lying next to her was a heavy poker.

Frederick went immediately to the telephone and rang Dr Harold Browne, who lived two houses away. Dr Browne hurried to the scene, and was met on the front drive by Frederick Wiltshaw. After glancing at the body, Dr Browne took Frederick into his sitting room and sat him down, trying to find words of comfort. 'Oh Doc,' the bereaved man replied, 'you always read about these things, but never think it will apply to you.'

The doctor returned to the hall and checked the body, taking care not to disturb anything. He concluded that Alice had been dead for less than an hour. His next step was to ring PC John Bigham at the village police house, telling him that Mrs Wiltshaw had met with a violent

Thomas Lockley, OBE, KPM, Chief Constable and a former Senior Detective Officer of the Staffordshire county force. He was a highly respected detective officer who successfully investigated a number of murders during his long and distinguished career. (Staffordshire Police Museum)

death. The time of the call was 6.25 pm and PC Bigham was at Estoril by 6.26 pm! After observing the state of the kitchen and taking a look at the body, the constable rang his senior officers, then asked Frederick Wiltshaw to check upstairs to see if there were any indications of a robbery. Frederick did so, but soon returned to say that he could see no signs of disturbance.

While they waited for other police officers to arrive, Dr Browne, wishing to take Frederick away from the immediate location of his wife's body, suggested that the two of them should go outside to the back of the house to take a look at Frederick's new car. Once outside, they saw that there were a couple of heifers trampling the garden. They had got into the garden by way of an open wicket gate. As the two men drove the cattle back through the gate, Dr Browne spotted a pair of bloodstained gloves discarded under an apple tree.

When they came back in, Superintendent Crook had arrived. He interviewed Frederick Wiltshaw and Dr Browne, checking what each had done after arriving at the scene. The doctor mentioned the gloves to him, and Frederick stated that they did not belong to any member of the household. At 7.15, Detective Chief Superintendent Tom Lockley, head of the Staffordshire CID, arrived, and after expressing his condolences to Frederick Wiltshaw, he took Superintendent Crook aside for a briefing. Being told that there seemed no signs of a robbery, Chief Superintendent Lockley now had to consider the possibility of a domestic killing. However, a couple of telephone calls soon proved that Frederick Wiltshaw's statements about his movements that afternoon were correct, and that he had only been alone in the house for less than a minute before calling Dr Browne. It was obvious that they were looking for an intruder. A police dog was brought in and followed a scent from the house, through the wicket gate and across the paddock. Unfortunately, the trail disappeared when it reached the road.

Having set up an incident room in a ground-floor study, officers began a detailed examination of the scene of the crime, and a start was made on tracing anyone – servants, neighbours, callers – who might have visited the house that day.

Frederick Wiltshaw was able to describe the domestic arrangements. He lived there with his 61 year old wife, Alice. Two daily maids, Ada Barlow and Florence Dorrell, worked in the house from 8.15 am to 3.30 pm, and a chauffeur-gardener, Roy Shenton, worked outside from 8 am until 5.30 pm. Mr Wiltshaw himself usually left for his pottery factory at 9.30 am and returned between 6.15 and 6.30 pm. Wilf Challinor leased three and a half acres of the grounds from the Wiltshaws as a market garden, and he and Albert Brookes usually worked there until 5 pm.

Checking with those involved, Tom Lockley established that the two maids had prepared the vegetables for the evening meal, leaving them in the saucepan for Mrs Wiltshaw to cook. They had left the house at 3.30 pm. The two market gardeners, Wilf and Albert, had finished work at 4.30 pm or just after. Roy Shenton had been busy working in the garden all day, seeing Mrs Wiltshaw from time to time. He heard her calling her dog to come for its food at about 5 o'clock. He had made a final wheelbarrow trip to the rubbish heap in the back garden at 5.15 pm and he was sure that the wicket gate was shut at this time. Roy had left on his motorbike at about 5.25 pm.

Tom Lockley mentally noted that Roy had worked at Estoril for only ten weeks, having replaced a Leslie Green who had been fired for unauthorised use of Mr Wiltshaw's car at weekends. Green was another person who would need questioning, so DS Robbins was dispatched to Green's home in Longton to interview him.

Tom established that Mrs Wiltshaw had phoned a friend at 5.05 pm and had spoken to her until 5.22 pm. Frederick Wiltshaw had arrived home to find his wife murdered at 6.18 pm. The killing had obviously occurred between 5.30 and 6.15 pm. A villager had seen a young man hanging about a path that led to the paddock at the rear of Estoril's back garden at about 5.45 pm. At 6 o'clock, two neighbours had seen that the wicket gate had been left open and some young cattle had wandered into the garden.

Meanwhile, investigations in the house had continued. The body was lying in a pool of blood close to the front door, the face mutilated and unrecognisable and the chest showing further wounds. A heavy steel poker lay by the body, bent out of shape. On the floor nearby were buttons from Mrs Wiltshaw's dress, her lower dentures, and pieces of a shattered earthenware jar.

In the kitchen, the floor and furniture were splashed with blood, as was the tablecloth. There were two large logs on the floor, both bloodstained and one with grey hair adhering to it. The faint outline of a shoe print was spotted, its tread forming slightly curving parallel lines. All this was carefully photographed.

In the sitting room, the recently delivered evening newspaper lay open on a chair. In the fireplace was a walking stick and Mrs Wiltshaw's handbag. The location of the walking stick puzzled the officers, as Frederick Wiltshaw had informed them that the heavy poker found by the body usually stood in this fireplace, and that the walking stick belonged in the hall.

Two other odd facts stood out. One was that Midge, the Wiltshaw's toy poodle, was a renowned loud 'barker', yet none of the neighbours had heard her barking between 5.30 and 6.15. The police had to wonder whether the killer was known to the dog. The other fact that did not fit was a report that a youth had been seen by neighbours running towards the paddock between 4.30 and 5 pm, although Mrs Wiltshaw was known to be still alive at 5.22 pm.

STAFFORDSHIRE & THE BLACK COUNTRY MURDER CASEBOOK

DS Robbins returned from Longton with the news that he had not found Leslie Green at home. Green's wife had said that Leslie had left her and gone off with a nurse he had met in Leeds. She believed that the couple had flown to Northern Ireland a fortnight earlier. Calls to the police in Leeds and Belfast seemed to confirm that the nurse and Green were in Belfast and had been there for some time. However, the next day it was realised that the Belfast police had not actually seen Green, and his name was reinstated on the possible suspect list. It became important that the man was found and interviewed, and Tom Lockley recommended to his Chief Constable that Scotland Yard be brought in.

At the post-mortem carried out by Professor J M Webster, it was established that the cause of death was shock and haemorrhage, the victim having been severely battered on the head and stabbed in the chest. The heavy steel poker, which had a barbed hook on the shaft, had been used for both purposes. Mrs Wiltshaw's fingers were severely bruised and she was wearing no rings. An attempt had been made to wrench a diamond RAF brooch from her dress, bending the clasp.

Given the attempt to take the diamond brooch and the absence of rings on the fingers, theft again seemed a strong possibility. Frederick Wiltshaw was asked to recheck the upstairs for anything missing. This time he reported that £3,000 worth of jewellery had gone from his wife's jewel case. When he had checked on the night of the murder, he had been in a state of shock. He had simply noted that the jewel case was in its usual place on the dressing table, and had not looked further. It now seemed certain that the killer was a thief. From a police viewpoint this was a useful bonus, since it opened a new line of inquiry, as well as giving a motive for the murder.

The local detectives were now joined by two Scotland Yard men, Detective Superintendent Reg Spooner and DS Ernie Millen. On the morning of Friday 18th July, they were taken to the murder location. Reg Spooner was particularly interested in the faint footprint, as well as the young man seen running from the premises. The search for this youth was extended into the nearby conurbation of Stoke-on-Trent, with full co-operation from the independent police force there. The search proved fruitless, however, and attention returned to finding the whereabouts of Leslie Green. It was learned that he had in fact left Belfast a week before the murder, and that he had several previous convictions for theft, though he had never shown any tendency to violence. A search of his marital home in Longton turned up a dress shirt, a jug and an ornament stolen from Estoril. Although these had no connection with the murder, having been stolen during the two years he had worked at Estoril, they did provide the police with a legitimate reason to arrest and hold Green when they found him.

The more Reg Spooner and Tom Lockley thought about the pattern of the murder, the more they wanted to interview the former chauffeur-gardener. Leslie Green knew the layout of the house from cleaning windows and moving furniture. He certainly knew the sitting room – the location of the poker – and the main bedroom where the jewellery was kept. He would have known that the way through the wicket gate in the back garden led to a public footpath. He knew the routine at Estoril: the fact that Alice Wiltshaw was usually alone in the house from 3.30 pm, when the maids left, until 6.15 pm when her husband returned. The toy poodle, Midge, was familiar with Green; she had not barked at the killer.

A possible scenario was built up. Leslie Green had sneaked into the house via the kitchen at 5.30 pm, planning to steal the jewellery from the bedroom while Alice Wiltshaw was reading the evening newspaper in the sitting room. On his way out, he was seen by Mrs Wiltshaw, who had gone to the kitchen to put on the vegetables. He knocked her down with a log and began to run away, before realising that she must have recognised him. He therefore pursued her to the hall and picked up the walking stick to finish her off, only to find it was inadequate for the task. He had remembered the heavy poker that stood in the sitting room, and fetched it. He returned to the hall, and there battered and stabbed Mrs Wiltshaw until she was dead.

At 9.15 am the next morning, a cool and confident Leslie Green walked into Longton police station and introduced himself as the man the police wanted to see. Reg Spooner, Tom Lockley and Ernie Millen went to Longton immediately to interview the man. Green confirmed his identity, and said that Mr Wiltshaw had sacked him for borrowing the car one weekend to visit his ladyfriend in Leeds. Asked where she was now, he replied that she was staying with relations in Birmingham prior to going home to Ireland.

At this stage Reg Spooner left the room to try to trace the nurse in Birmingham, and Tom Lockley continued the interview. Leslie Green freely admitted that he had used the name L Wiltshaw of Barlaston when booking in at a hotel in Leeds.

He was quite sure how he had spent the afternoon of Wednesday 16th July. He had been in Stafford at the Station Hotel, after travelling up from London in the morning. His original intention was to travel on

Leslie Green. (*Express & Star*)

to Longton to try to patch up his marriage, but he had got into a serious drinking session with four men, one of them the manager of the hotel, until 3.30 pm, when they went into the dining room for a meal. After eating, they went back into the bar until 5 pm. Green had walked into the town centre, found a park, and fallen asleep on a bench for a while. When he woke up at 5.45, he had returned to the Station Hotel, washed, changed his shirt, and had another meal in the dining room. He left the hotel at 6.45 pm and caught the 7.07 train from Stafford to Leeds. He was sure the ticket collector would remember him, as they had had a conversation about air flights to Ireland.

After this interview, Green was taken to the police station at Stone, where he was examined by Dr C Arthur, a police surgeon, who took blood samples, plus hair and nail clippings. Asked about abrasions on his right wrist and hand, and a cut on his left thumb, Green replied, 'I fell down on Ilkley Moor a fortnight ago.'

By this time, Green's girlfriend had been traced to an address in Brierley Hill. She told the police that she had no idea that Leslie Green, whom she knew as Terry, was married. She said that they were engaged and marriage banns had been published while they were in Belfast. She was unable or unwilling to give any further information, but the police in Leeds had spoken to two of her former colleagues who were certain that when Green had visited the girl on the evening of Wednesday 16th July – the day of the murder – and had shown them two diamond rings. Their description of the two rings matched that of the rings stolen from the dead fingers of Mrs Alice Wiltshaw.

Tom Lockley decided to test out the information on Green, saying that the police believed he had given two diamond rings to his fiancée, rings which matched the description of those stolen from Estoril. Without a trace of nervousness, Leslie Green replied that they might be from Estoril but they had been given to him in Leeds at lunchtime on the day after the murder by two men he knew only as Charlie and Lorenzo. He had given the rings to his fiancée, but she had later returned them to him and he had thrown them in the river.

In a new statement, he also said that at the time he was working at Estoril, Lorenzo had asked him if there was jewellery kept in the house and that he had replied, 'I suppose so.' He said he now believed that Lorenzo and Charlie might have killed Mrs Wiltshaw. However, the police knew from the witnesses in Leeds that Leslie Green had the two rings in his possession on the evening of the murder, 12 hours before Lorenzo and Charlie were supposed to have given them to him.

The only thing now keeping Leslie Green from being charged with the murder was his alibi. He had claimed that he had been away from the Station Hotel in Stafford between 5 pm and 5.45 pm, when he was sleeping on a park bench, but when Ernie Millen questioned Geoff Farr, the manager of the hotel, the times were somewhat different. Mr Farr confirmed that Leslie Green had spent the afternoon drinking with him, but said that they had finished their meal by 4 pm, not 5 pm. He stated that Green then left the hotel and did not return until 6.30 pm, not 5.45 pm as he had claimed. This meant that Leslie Green now had 90 minutes when he had no alibi, not the 45 minutes previously thought. Was it possible for anyone to get to Barlaston from Stafford, commit the murder, and then return, in one and a half hours?

Tom Lockley was determined to find out. Could Green have stolen a car from the vicinity of the Station Hotel and returned before it was missed? Then a thought struck him; he rang the railway station and asked about afternoon trains between Stafford and Barlaston. He was told that there was a train that left Stafford at 5.10 and arrived at Barlaston at 5.33. A return journey was possible, catching the 6.05 from Barlaston, arriving back in Stafford at 6.27. Was the whole thing feasible?

Without telling his colleagues, Tom went to Stafford railway station that afternoon and caught the 5.10 train. The train was held up and did not arrive at Barlaston until 5.40. The murderer would not have walked openly down the main street, so Tom devised a route that involved going over the station fence – easy at an unmanned station – and across fields. He entered the wicket gate at the back of Estoril and walked up to the house. Checking his watch, he found that it was 5.47 pm. He calculated that a seven-minute return walk back to the station, arriving there in time to catch the 6.05, would leave him 11 minutes, time enough to commit a robbery and a murder. Yes, it *was* feasible! Leslie Green's alibi was broken.

At Leslie Green's trial, further telling circumstantial evidence was forthcoming. The cut on Green's left thumb matched a cut in the glove found by Dr Browne in the garden at Estoril. One of Green's shoes had tread that corresponded with the faint print on the floor at the murder scene. An RAF raincoat, seen in Green's possession by the manager of the Station Hotel on the evening of the murder, was found abandoned on the train in which Green had left Stafford. This coat belonged to Frederick Wiltshaw and had been stolen from Estoril on the day of the murder. Moreover, it had bloodstains on the right sleeve that matched Green's injured right wrist.

Not everything fitted neatly, of course. The youth seen running at the back of the house at 4.30 pm on the day of the murder was never identified, and the bulk of the jewellery was never recovered. However, the stolen diamond rings, torn from the dead woman's fingers, were eventually found hidden in a flat where Leslie Green and his fiancée had stayed.

The evidence, although circumstantial, was overwhelming. Above all, Superintendent Lockley had, through determination and inspiration, shattered the accused man's alibi and proved that he had the opportunity to commit the crime. He had had 11 minutes to murder his former employer.

Leslie Green was found guilty, and was hanged on 23rd December 1952. On the day of the execution, Tom Lockley was surprised to receive a letter that ended: 'So long, enemy – enemies perhaps but in many respects, gratefully yours, Leslie Green.'

11

SUICIDE
VIA MURDER

The Murder of Donald Lainton near Uttoxeter
February 1955

Donald Lainton was a 28 year old married man, who worked for a firm of insurance brokers in Stockport. On Friday 25th February 1955, he had a business appointment in Sutton Coldfield. Initially doubtful about making the journey because of heavy snow, he rang the AA and was told that the main roads were passable. However, when he got to Staffordshire the snow was even worse, and he phoned to cancel his appointment.

In the village of Great Haywood, he pulled into the car park of the Coach and Horses public house, and went in to try to get a hot meal. He was disappointed to find that the pub did not serve food, but as Donald sat having a quiet drink, a man who had been playing the piano came over to his table and told him that he knew of a nearby pub where meals were available. He offered to show Donald the way to the place, and after they had finished their drinks, the two men left the pub and got into Donald Lainton's car.

At 1.45 that afternoon, a green saloon car was noticed in a lane leading to Birchen Bower Farm, Willslock, near Uttoxeter. Bernard Bettson, the son-in-law of the farm's owner, could see that the car was stuck in a snowdrift. He watched as a man came round the car and began to rock it backward and forward, as if trying to move it. A little later, he observed that the man had gone, but the car was still there. At about 3 pm, Mr. Bettson's wife, Elizabeth, went to have a closer look at the vehicle. There was blood on the car door, and when she looked inside, she saw a briefcase on the back seat and what looked liked a man's knees on the floor of the car. Luckily, a milk tanker appeared alongside them, and Mrs Bettson asked the driver and his mate – Ray

Ward and Jack Johnson – for help. They checked the car and saw a
body under some overcoats. They closed the car door and drove the
milk tanker to the Red Cow pub to phone for help.

Quite fortuitously, an ambulance crewed by Ken Fallows and Alan
Goodall was on its way from Burton to Uttoxeter. When they reached
the scene, they stopped and found that the man in the car – Donald
Lainton – was gravely wounded and bleeding. They got the injured
man into the ambulance and, despite the snow-covered road, decided
to take him to Stafford General Infirmary. 'We used the ambulance like
a snow-plough,' Ken told me. 'We must have pushed a ton of snow all
the way to Stafford.' At the hospital the staff concluded that the man
had been stabbed, and sent for the police, who kept a bedside vigil all
night. However, the injured man died without being able to give them a
description of his assailant.

A post-mortem, conducted by Professor J M Webster, established that
death had been caused by shock and haemorrhage, following stab
wounds which had lacerated the brain and right lung. Considering that
the most serious stab wound had gone through the man's eye and
pierced his brain, it was incredible that Donald Lainton had not been
killed outright. Besides the numerous wounds to the head, neck and
chest, there were some injuries to the back of the right hand, indicating
that the murdered man had been trying to defend himself.

Chief Superintendent Tom Lockley immediately ordered road checks
to be mounted on all vehicles entering or leaving Uttoxeter. He
appealed for information from anyone who might have given a lift to a
stranger in the area between 1 pm and 5 pm on the afternoon of 25th
February. At this stage, it was thought that Donald Lainton might have
been murdered by a hitchhiker, and that robbery was the most likely
motive. The murder squad from Scotland Yard was called in, and
Detective Superintendent Stephen Glander and DS Bruce were sent to
help the Staffordshire CID investigate the murder.

It was not a lengthy investigation. On Monday 28th February, at the
magistrates' court in Uttoxeter, Frederick Arthur Cross, a 33 year old
concrete-moulder from Farley, Great Haywood, was charged with the
murder of Donald Lainton. He was remanded in custody until 24th
March, when the committal proceedings began.

David Prys-Jones, the prosecuting counsel, described to the court
how on the afternoon of 25th February Mr and Mrs Bettson had found
the car with the mortally wounded Donald Lainton lying inside. He said
that the murdered man was an insurance agent and was driving a car

provided by his employers, a firm of Stockport insurance brokers. He described how Lainton had tried to obtain a meal at a public house in Great Haywood. The licensee, Mrs Lilian Lawson, had heard him talking to a local man, Fred Cross, who had earlier been playing the piano in the bar. She had seen the two men leave together in a green Ford Prefect car.

The prosecution told the court that after the assault on Donald Lainton, Cross had walked for some miles, then entered the village post office in Kingstone and asked if he could hire a taxi to take him back to Great Haywood. He could not get a taxi, but managed to hitch a lift in a lorry driven by Harry Bridge. Mr Bridge dropped Cross near the Coach and Horses, and saw him fetch out a bicycle from behind a phone box. Cross cycled to his home, a Nissen hut at Farley, where he burnt the mackintosh he had been wearing.

The next day, Saturday 26th February, Cross travelled to the home of his mother-in-law in Alcester, Warwickshire. On the evening of Sunday 27th February, a member of the Warwickshire police had gone to the house where Cross was staying. He saw Fred Cross, who said, 'I know what you want me for. Don't say any more. I will tell you outside. Don't upset the old lady.' Cross was taken to Stratford-upon-Avon police station, where he told the police that he had stabbed Donald Lainton with part of an old pair of scissors, throwing it into a field after the assault.

He denied taking any money from the dead man, insisting that robbery was not the motive for his crime. In a bizarre but chilling statement, he explained that his wife had left him for another man on New Year's Day, taking their two children with her. He discovered that she had been seeing the man for two years. He had written to her to ask her to come back to him, but she had not replied. He brooded for a while, and made up his mind to commit suicide. He had even gone to Stafford and bought a tin of rat poison for the purpose, but then lacked the courage to take it. When he met Donald Lainton in the public house on the fatal Friday afternoon, he had suddenly conceived the idea that if he killed his new acquaintance, he would be hanged for the crime and thus achieve his wish to die.

Cross said that after he and Donald Lainton had left the pub together, they had driven for some distance before he told Lainton to turn into a drive on the left-hand side of the road. When the car had stopped, he had taken part of a pair of scissors from his mackintosh pocket and struck the man several times in the head and chest. Lainton had put his hands up to protect himself, but Cross had 'just gone berserk'. The accused man said that he could remember getting behind the steering wheel and driving along the road. He stopped the car and sat, trying to think what to do next. Then he drove on again until he reached a turning on the left, and drove into it. While he was looking back along the road, his arm must have slipped and the car went off the road. Frightened, he got out and tried to get the car back onto the road by pulling the rear bumper with his hands. He failed to free the car and decided to leave it.

Frederick Cross, who was not legally represented in court, said that he was not a bit sorry for himself, and that he was not worth being sorry for. 'But', he added, 'I am sorry for the man, and I wish I had known before I did this that he was married. I do not want to live. I have nothing to live for.'

Cross was sent for trial at Stafford Assizes, and appeared before Mr Justice Gorman on 5th July 1955. The trial was an incredibly short one. When informed by the judge that if he required a lawyer to put his case, one would be provided, Cross – who was slightly deaf – failed to hear what was being said. When the clerk of the assize, Mr J Tumin, repeated the judge's offer to arrange legal representation, Cross answered, 'No, I want to plead guilty.'

Mr Justice Gorman continued, 'You do understand, don't you, that if you plead guilty to this charge, I have no alternative but to pass sentence? Do you fully understand?' The clerk again had to repeat the judge's words, and Cross answered, 'Yes, sir.'

The clerk then told Cross that he stood convicted on his own confession of wilful murder, and asked if he had anything to say which might indicate why the court should not give him judgement to die. Cross replied, 'That is what I wish.' Mr Justice Gorman then passed sentence of death. The whole trial had taken eight minutes.

Frederick Arthur Cross was hanged in Winson Green prison on 25th July 1955, exactly five months after his crime. He had achieved his aim of committing suicide by committing murder, though the real price was paid by Donald Lainton's widow and baby son.

12

THE
FATAL TRIANGLE

The Murder of Mary Elizabeth Walton at Rudyard
February 1963

On Saturday 9th February 1963, bus driver Reuben Austin was working on the route between the Potteries town of Tunstall and Mow Cop, the high Staffordshire village which lies on the border with Cheshire. It was an icy cold day, with frozen snow lying by the side of the roads, as the bus climbed to the village. Reuben first noticed a red Mini-traveller estate car parked in the High Street at Mow Cop at 1 pm; it was still there, parked without lights, on his next visit at 6.50 pm. When he returned to Mow Cop at 9.15, the vehicle was still there, and Reuben decided to investigate. He parked his bus, went over to the car and took a look in through the iced-up windows. Lying behind the back seats was the body of a woman. Reuben hurried to a nearby café and rang for the police.

PC Everett was the first to arrive. He found that the side doors of the estate car were locked, but he was able to force open the rear door. He saw that the woman was dead and had suffered severe head injuries. Other officers arrived and an investigation began. It was quickly established that the ignition and car door keys were missing. The parked car had first been observed shortly after 11 pm on the Friday night when its headlights were on, though they had obviously failed during the night or the following day.

A check on the registration number – 880 WEH – proved that the red Mini estate was the property of Mrs Mary Elizabeth Walton of Newcastle-under-Lyme, who had been reported missing during the Saturday afternoon. Early on the Sunday morning, the body in the car was identified as that of Mrs Walton by Dr Scott, her family doctor.

A post-mortem conducted by Home Office pathologist Dr George

Staffordshire police search the icy streams and woods for clues in the Mary Walton case.
(H Jones Allcock/Shirley Palin)

Bernard Manning found several lacerations on the back of the head, corresponding to numerous skull fractures. At least eight blows had been struck, all with considerable force. There was also a curved shallow wound on the bridge of the nose, surrounded by bruising, and grazing on one thumb and both legs. Death had been caused by cerebral haemorrhage associated with the injuries to the head.

The police established that Mrs Walton, who was 52, had been a home help supervisor employed by Staffordshire County Council. Her husband Frank was the business director of a firm in Hanley. Frank Walton told the police that he had gone to work at 9 am on Friday 8th February and returned home at 5.30 pm. He had last seen his wife at 6.30 pm when they had both left the house, in separate cars. He had driven in his Rover to visit his parents who lived in Audley; Mrs Walton had gone in her own car to visit friends. When he returned at 8.30 pm, his wife was not there and she did not come home that night. The next day, he began to ring various family friends to ask if they had seen her. He learned from Dr and Mrs Scott that his wife had called on them at

Police removing bloodstained ice at Rudyard. (H Jones Allcock/Shirley Palin)

7 pm on the previous evening, but had only stayed 20 minutes. Shortly after Frank Walton's call, Dr Scott phoned the police to report Mary Walton missing.

Police officers began to circulate a questionnaire to residents of Mow Cop and Kidsgrove, asking: (1) Where were you after 7.30 on Friday evening? (2) Did you pass along High Street, Mow Cop? (3) Did you see anything suspicious? (4) Did you see anyone about in the High Street vicinity whom you did not know? (5) Did you see any signs of a fight involving a woman, or hear anything suspicious? (6) Did you see a red Morris Mini-traveller vehicle, registration number 880 WEH, moving along or stationary? If so, where? (7) Did you use a bus in the vicinity of Mow Cop between 7.30 and 11.30 on that evening? If so, did you notice anyone get on whom you did not know or who aroused your suspicions? (8) Did you know Mrs Walton? (9) Did she ever call at your house? (10) Was she due to call at your house?

The questionnaire was very general, but it was not long before the questions became more specific. Detectives were now asking motorists if they had given a lift to a woman in the Mow Cop or Congleton areas around midnight on Friday 8th February. Police activity soon switched to the village of Rudyard, about two miles north-west of Leek, from where samples of bloodstained ice and frozen snow were taken away for forensic examination. The police interest was concentrated on a bungalow known as The Willows, the home of 34 year old Gwen Massey and her elderly grandparents.

Gwen had lived in Rudyard for the whole of her life, first in her parents' home, then moving to the bungalow in Green Lane to live with her grandparents. She became a student nurse at the North Stafford-shire Royal Infirmary, and was doing well, but gave up the post after a year to concentrate on caring for her elderly grandparents.

Her whole existence would have been restricted to the village were it not for an exceptional talent. Gwen had a wonderful singing voice. At the age of three, she was singing in the village Methodist chapel. At her primary school in Leek, the teachers were soon aware that Gwen's beautiful but untutored voice deserved special attention, and she was advised to seek a specialist voice tutor. She enrolled as a pupil of a well-known singing teacher in Stoke-on-Trent, Miss Lucy Hall, and it was there that she first met Frank Walton. Gwen Massey began many years of hard, disciplined training and, at her first music festival, held at the Central Hall in Longton, she won her class. In the years that followed, Gwen sang at chapels in Staffordshire and Cheshire, and competed in music festivals throughout the north of England. At the prestigious Lytham St Anne's festival, near Blackpool, Gwen won the soprano solo class and was then judged the most outstanding performer of the festival.

She often appeared at musical events in the nearby towns of Leek, Biddulph and Congleton, and it was at Biddulph in January 1959 that Gwen and Frank sang a duet together. Afterwards, Frank asked Gwen to go for a drink with him. Frank was 17 years older than Gwen, but

Gwen Massey. (H Jones Allcock/Shirley Palin)

their mutual love of music led to them becoming good friends. The friendship ripened into a deeper affection and, despite the fact that Frank Walton had a wife and family at home, the pair became lovers.

The love affair continued for four years, until the autumn of 1962, when Frank's wife discovered that he was being unfaithful. She did not ask the identity of his girlfriend, but demanded that he put an end to the liaison. Frank, who had never intended to leave his wife and family, agreed and told Gwen that he could no longer see her. Since then the lovers had met only once. This was in September, when they had gone for a drive and sat and discussed the situation. After that, their only contact was by phone, Frank ringing Gwen regularly from work.

On Sunday 10th February, Detective Sergeant Ken Newton went to Gwen Massey's home at 4.20 am, accompanied by another police officer, and questioned her. Gwen made a statement about her affair with Frank Walton, stating that they had broken it off before Christmas by mutual agreement, after Frank's wife had found out. Gwen said that on Friday 8th February, she had been shopping in Leek with her mother between 3 pm and 5 pm. The next day, at about 1 pm, Frank had phoned her to say that his wife was missing; he asked Gwen if she knew anyone who might have spoken to his wife on the phone, but Gwen had said she did not. Frank had phoned again at teatime to tell Gwen that his wife was to be reported missing. Gwen told DS Newton categorically that she had never met Mrs Walton.

On Tuesday 12th February, DS Newton called by appointment at Gwen's home and took her to Congleton police station, where she was questioned by Newton and Detective Chief Superintendent Turner. She was asked about a red Mini that had been parked outside her home on the night of Mrs Walton's death. Gwen denied any knowledge of this, saying that people often parked there and that a local farmer owned such a vehicle. She had heard no suspicious noises that evening, and had gone to bed at about 10 pm. She had neither made nor received any telephone calls.

In a further statement made to DS Newton at 9.45 pm on Saturday 16th February, Gwen Massey changed her story, saying that on the evening of 8th February, she had hard a dog barking outside at about 8 pm. She went outside and found the body of a woman lying on the steps. She could detect no signs of life, and in a blind panic she had tried, unsuccessfully, to lift the woman's body, intending to put it into the Mini-traveller. She had found the car keys in the vehicle, but it would not start. Leaving the body on the steps, she had run indoors, and had heard a vehicle start up at about 10 pm. She had no idea who the woman was. The next morning she had noticed blood on the ice on the steps. She had used a spade to chip the ice up and had disposed of it on the other side of the road, then poured hot water over the steps. She had been horrified at the whole event. She had not told the truth at previous interviews because she did not want to drag Frank Walton's name into the affair. The statement ended: 'I have been out of my mind not knowing what to do. I had nothing to do with this terrible thing. I never made any telephone calls.'

At midnight, Gwen was taken to Congleton police station where she sat for some time with her head in her hands. She complained of a headache and was given two tablets and a glass of water. Nothing further took place until 2 am when a woman officer, Police Sergeant Edith Allen, arrived from Crewe. Gwen answered further questions from 2 am until 5.15 am when she made a fourth statement, admitting that she had in fact killed Mary Walton with a hammer, and adding, 'I just didn't mean it. I never thought it would end up like that. I never dreamed anything like that would happen.'

Gwendoline Massey appeared at a special county magistrates' court in Congleton on Monday 18th February, charged with the murder of Mary Walton, and was remanded in custody. The committal hearing was held before magistrates in Congleton in early April, and the prosecuting counsel, David Prys-Jones, alleged that Gwen had inflicted a number of blows with a hammer on Mrs Walton's head after a quarrel, and had then tried to dispose of the body by putting it into Mrs Walton's own car and abandoning it in Mow Cop. He described the finding of the body by bus driver Reuben Austin, and outlined the affair between Gwen Massey and Frank Walton which had ended when Mary Walton found out about it.

Mr Prys-Jones said that what happened to Mrs Walton between 7.30 pm on 8th February, when she left the home of Dr Scott, and the time of her death was a matter of some conjecture. However, at about 8 pm Mrs Buxton, who lived at the farm next door to Gwen Massey's bungalow, saw two cars driving along the road. One of them, Gwen Massey's Morris Minor, turned in towards the garage where it was usually kept. The other car stopped just outside the farm gate. It was still parked there at 9 pm but had gone by 10.15 pm, so it had been parked outside Gwen Massey's home for about two hours. The prosecution alleged that this vehicle was Mary Walton's red Mini-traveller, and that at some time during those two hours, Gwen Massey killed her. She then put the body into the back of the estate car, drove it 11 miles to Mow Cop and then walked the 11 miles home. Four witnesses saw a woman walking between Mow Cop and Congleton between 11 pm and midnight. All of them would remember the event, as it was very unusual to see a woman walking on these lonely roads late on a bitterly cold and snowy night in such conditions.

The prosecution then referred to the finding of a quantity of bloodstained ice and frozen snow in a copse, over a farm wall opposite Miss Massey's bungalow. Further traces of blood were found on the bungalow path, and forensic tests showed the blood to be type A, the same type as that of the murdered woman. A hammer head, four inches long and pointed at one end, had been found in the coal shed of the bungalow. The shaft of the hammer was missing and the metal head showed signs of having been 'subjected to heat'.

Mr Prys-Jones also referred to witnesses who had seen two cars in the car park of the Plough Hotel in Endon at 7.30 pm on the night of the murder. Two women were sitting in one of the cars, talking; then both cars drove off one behind the other towards Leek. He suggested that these women were Gwen Massey and Mary Walton, who had met by appointment, then driven to Gwen's home in Rudyard, where later that evening the murder had been committed.

Reuben Austin gave evidence about how he had discovered the body, and Dr Manning described his findings at the post-mortem. On being shown the hammer head, he agreed that it could have caused the wounds to the face and the back of the head of the dead woman. He added that Mrs Walton had been dead for approximately 24 hours before he examined the body at 1 am on Sunday 10th February; it was his opinion that she had died three or four hours after the attack.

Tom Whittaker said that he had seen a woman walking away from Mow Cop towards Congleton as he was taking his girlfriend home on his motorbike at 11.30 pm on the night of 8th February, and again as he returned 20 minutes later. He identified Gwen Massey as the woman he had seen. In answer to questions from Mr Eifion Roberts, the defence counsel, Mr Whittaker agreed that on the first occasion he had only seen the woman from the back and that the collar of her fur coat was turned up. John Gallimore gave evidence of having seen a woman walking between Mow Cop and Congleton, and he too identified her as Gwen Massey. He agreed with the defence counsel that his car windows might have been partially frosted up.

Other witnesses, including a dairyman, a garage owner and an off-duty police constable, said that they had seen a red Mini estate parked in the gateway of the farm adjoining Gwen Massey's home on the evening of the murder. Neil Pickford said that at 9.30 pm he had gone to the farm to play cards with the farmer, Michael Buxton. He had seen the Mini estate parked in the gateway, and had also seen a woman on the path of the bungalow. He had only seen her lower half and was unable to identify her. When Michael Buxton drove him home later, the vehicle had gone.

Michael Buxton – Gwen Massey's cousin and neighbour – gave evidence that he had visited the bungalow between 6.30 and 6.45 pm, but Gwen was not there. A few days later he had noticed bloodstained pieces of ice on a tip across the road and had informed the police.

On 4th April, the third day of the trial, the defence counsel requested that the rest of the evidence – believed to be related to Gwen Massey's four statements to the police – should be heard in camera. There was no objection from the prosecution, and the chairman of the magistrates, Miss E A Ward, ordered that the press and public should leave. This part of the proceedings lasted six hours, but at 3.50 pm the public were readmitted. The magistrates retired for two minutes before deciding that a prima-facie case had been made, and Gwen Massey was committed for trial at the next assizes.

The full trial took place in May before Mr Justice Ashworth, with W L Mars-Jones QC leading for the prosecution. The defence was led by Emlyn Hooson QC, the Liberal MP. Much of the evidence was identical to that given in the magistrates' court. Frank Walton was questioned at some length about his affair with Gwen Massey, and in answer to questions from Emlyn Hooson, he told the court that Gwen had seemed content with her position as his mistress, and had never asked him to seek a divorce. She had never shown any hostility towards his wife. He agreed with the defence counsel that he had been the jealous partner in the affair, and would have resented Gwen having any friendship with another man. He admitted that, even after the reconciliation with his wife, he spoke to Gwen on the telephone every day because he was still in love with her.

After Margaret Buxton had given evidence about seeing the red Mini estate parked outside Gwen's bungalow, she was asked about occasions when her son Philip cut his fingers and had gone next door to 'Aunty Gwen' to have them dressed. She told the court that this had happened twice, once in January and once on a Sunday sometime later. She agreed that blood had dripped from Philip's fingers as he went to the bungalow, but added that the police had taken a sample of Philip's blood to compare with the blood found after the 8th February.

In the absence of the jury, who were sent to wait in another room for two hours, the judge heard legal arguments from the defence counsel on the admissibility of certain evidence. Before the jury were readmitted, Mr Justice Ashworth warned the press and public – who had remained in the courtroom – not to discuss any of the points that had been mentioned.

DS Kenneth Newton gave evidence that Gwen Massey had confessed the murder to him in the early hours of the morning at Congleton police station. After he had left the room for a while, he returned and was told by Superintendent Rimmer that Gwen 'wants to tell you something'. He stated that she had leaned on his shoulder and said in a quiet voice, 'Oh, it was horrible. You have no idea. I can't remember a lot about it really.' The sergeant alleged that Gwen had described how she had struck the woman down with a hammer, and said, 'It wouldn't have happened except for her nagging him.' Questioned by the defence, DS Newton agreed that, apart from two periods of 10 and 45 minutes, Gwen Massey had been questioned by himself and Sergeant Morris from 2 am until 5.15 am. He stated that over a period of several days he had questioned her for a total of between 10 and 15 hours. He agreed that she had been distressed and crying when she made her final statement. When asked about the previous character of the accused, Sergeant Newton said that from his inquiries, he had learned that Gwen had been a woman of good character with a reputation for being kind and helpful. He agreed that she was fond of children, and children loved her, and that she was regarded as a good-natured person.

Superintendent Rimmer gave evidence that, at about 5.20 am on 17th February, Gwen Massey had said to him, 'I don't want to die', and that he had assured her that, even if she was responsible for Mrs Walton's death, the death sentence would not be imposed. He denied that he had started this conversation by telling the accused that she was too young to die. He also denied telling her that if she made another statement, she would be allowed to go home. Emlyn Hooson put it to Superintendent Rimmer that Miss Massey was afraid of him. The superintendent replied, 'I wouldn't say that', but agreed that Sergeant Newton had got on with Gwen Massey better than he had.

On the morning of Wednesday 29th May, the fourth day of the trial, David Prys-Jones addressed the jury for 40 minutes, and alleged that all of the evidence pointed in one direction, to the unquestionable guilt of the accused. He believed that when Superintendent Rimmer had told Gwen Massey that the offence did not carry the death penalty, this news had opened the floodgates of her conscience and allowed her to make her final statement. He said that the superintendent had been quite right to point this out to the accused, who was evidently under a misapprehension. Gwen Massey's final statement had the ring of truth about it.

In his address to the jury, Emlyn Hooson said that this was far from the open-and-shut case alleged by the prosecution. There were matters which should cause them great anxiety. He asked them to consider whether the savage and forceful injuries inflicted on Mrs Walton could have been caused by any woman, let alone by Gwen Massey, an attractive woman of good character who had never been in trouble before. On the matter of Gwen's final statement, he expressed surprise at the comment by the police that Gwen Massey had merely been 'invited' to go to the police station as a witness, and was never taken into custody. This meant that she had never been cautioned or advised that she need not say anything. If the jury had any doubts that Gwen Massey's final statement was a free and voluntary one, they should reject it completely.

In his summing-up, Mr Justice Ashworth told the jury that they had to decide whether it was Mrs Walton's car that witnesses had seen at Endon and at Rudyard. They also had to decide who the woman was who was seen walking on the road on that Friday night. He read out Gwen Massey's four statements, pointing out that if the fourth one was true, then the previous three could not be. The judge reminded the jury that at 5 am Superintendent Rimmer and a woman police officer had been left alone with Gwen Massey. They might think it 'unfortunate to say the least' that Superintendent Rimmer should then send the policewoman out to make tea, leaving him alone with the accused. The interview with the superintendent was one of very, very great importance, as it led to the final statement. The judge said that the two police sergeants must have been gifted with startlingly good memories, as they had given evidence without reference to any notes. However, their evidence had not been challenged.

After the judge's summing-up, the jury retired at 3.45 pm to consider their verdict, returning after one and a quarter hours to say that they had found the accused guilty of murdering Mary Walton. Mr Justice Ashworth addressed Gwen Massey, telling her: 'For the crime of which you have been convicted the law provides only one penalty, namely imprisonment for life, and that is the sentence I pass on you.'

After the trial, Gwen Massey's brother told reporters: 'Although we were half prepared for this, the verdict was a terrible shock.' Gwen's cousin, Michael Buxton – whose evidence of finding bloodstained ice had formed part of the prosecution case – said, 'My wife thought up to the last minute that Gwen would be acquitted. It is the verdict of guilty which upsets us as much as the sentence.' He said later that Gwen had been a caring and affectionate 'aunty' to his children.

Margaret Buxton revealed that she had taken letters from the children every time she visited Gwen on remand in Strangeways prison. She said that Gwen had read them avidly but, under prison regulations, was not allowed to keep them. One particularly poignant letter from Philip asked Gwen to try to get home for his birthday. Margaret said that her children had always loved Gwen and that, whatever had happened, she did not intend that they should change their opinion of her.

13

THE
A34 CHILD MURDER

The Murder of Christine Darby on Cannock Chase
August 1967

On the afternoon of Saturday 19th August 1967, seven year old Christine Darby was out playing with two friends, Nicholas Baldry and Alwyn Isaacs. The two boys had called at Christine's house in Camden Street, Walsall, at about 1 o'clock, and the three youngsters had wandered around the neighbourhood, looking for other friends to play with. All their playmates seemed to be out. At 2.20 pm, they called at a house in Corporation Street, but the friend who lived there had gone to the pictures.

The three wandered back to Camden Street, but as they turned the corner, a car pulled up. The driver wound down the passenger window and asked them the way to Caldmore Green. Nicki, Alwyn and Christine pointed to their right, indicating the direction he had to go. The driver opened the front passenger door and said to Christine, 'Would you please get in and show me the way?' Seven year old Christine climbed in, and smiled at her two friends as the car reversed out of Camden Street into Corporation Street. The two boys smiled back somewhat enviously, but were very surprised when the car moved off; it was not travelling towards Caldmore Green, but in the opposite direction.

Realising that something was very wrong, they raced to Christine's house and told her grandmother that a man had driven off with Christine. Mrs Henrietta Darby ran with the boys to the spot where Christine had got into the car, but there was nothing to be seen. Christine's mother Lilian came out of the house to be told the news. The two distressed women ran round the corner to Coxshall's off-licence where the nearest phone was situated, and Mr Coxshall dialled 999.

The call was received at Wolverhampton police station at 2.52 pm. Sergeant John Warren immediately dispatched a patrol car to Christine's home, and alerted the Walsall police station. Eight year old Nicki Baldry was taken on a ride around the streets of Walsall to see if he could spot the car that had abducted his friend. Road blocks were set up, and neighbouring forces alerted.

Incidents of children being taken away in strange cars are always taken extremely seriously, but the West Midlands and Staffordshire police forces had another ominous reason to treat this case with the utmost urgency: in 1965, two young girls had been kidnapped by a lone car driver. Although the abductions had occurred three months apart, both bodies were found lying together in an isolated lane on Cannock Chase, an area of 100 square miles of forest, heathland and bracken.

Little wonder, then, that the disappearance of Christine Darby had set alarm bells ringing for the police. Walsall, like the homes of the two earlier victims, lay on the A34 road to Cannock Chase, and Christine was about the same age as the two murdered girls.

Nicki Baldry was questioned by WPC Mary Amos. Some of the information he gave her about the man's age and the make of his car was understandably vague, but one clue Nicki gave proved of great value. When the car driver had asked the way to Caldmore Green, he had used the local pronunciation: 'Karma Green'. Anyone from outside the area would surely have pronounced Caldmore as it is written. Nicki's clear and definite memory of the driver's pronunciation of Karma Green convinced the police that they were seeking a local man, certainly someone from the Black Country and probably from Walsall itself.

All police leave in Walsall was stopped, and a house-to-house check began, working outwards from Camden Street. Every member of each house was asked to look at Christine's photograph and to read her description: Christine was 3 ft 9 in with blue eyes and dark brown, shoulder-length hair cut in a fringe. She was wearing a white T-shirt with a floral pattern, dark blue trousers, black plimsolls, white ankle socks and a blue nylon underskirt. Everyone was asked if they had seen the girl in a car, or if they had seen a strange car in the area on Saturday 19th. A hundred police officers were involved, and neighbours of Lilian and Henrietta Darby formed their own search parties to look in sheds, backyard coal bunkers and on waste ground throughout the town.

The other area to be searched was Cannock Chase. PC Arthur Ellis was one of six mounted police officers searching roads that led off the A34 at the southern edge of the Chase. Arthur and a colleague were riding along the Rugeley to Penkridge road about three miles north of Cannock, when he spotted something white hanging on a tree branch. Closer examination showed it to be a pair of small white knickers; on the next day, Monday, Henrietta Darby identified them by cotton she had used to repair them. A child's plimsoll, its lace still tied in a bow, was discovered by forestry worker Jim Leech, and this was also identified as Christine's by her mother and grandmother.

The main police activity immediately switched from Walsall to Cannock, and a second HQ was set up in a large house formerly used by the DSS. As well as the normal telephone and radio links, closed circuit television was also installed so that documents could be read simultaneously in both the Cannock and Walsall incident rooms.

Five hundred police officers, together with 50 police dogs and 350 servicemen, were drafted in for a mass search of Cannock Chase. Ominously, the search was beginning less than three miles from Mansty Gully, where the bodies of the two earlier victims had been discovered 20 months earlier. The searchers worked steadily, shoulder to shoulder, using sticks and billhooks to hack down the brambles and bracken, and passing any objects found back to a central point. The 400 items of women's underwear they discovered led to some caustic jokes. This was not callous levity, but desperate 'gallows humour', intended to stave off thoughts of the terrible nature of the task in which they were all engaged. Police frogmen began to search the flooded gravel pits, and plans were being made to enrol 5,000 civilian volunteers on the following Monday, a bank holiday.

The volunteers, however, were not to be needed. At 5.40 pm on Tuesday 22nd August, the body of Christine Darby was found. One hundred and twenty-five new recruits from the Staffordshire Regiment had been given a day's respite from basic training to help with the search. They were sent to a location known as Plantation 110, and it was there that Private Michael Blundred discovered Christine's partially clothed body hidden in the ferns.

Michael's first impression was of a bundle of clothes lying at the foot of a tree, but he quickly realised that it was the body of the little girl for whom he and his companions were looking. He blew a blast on his whistle, and the search for Christine Darby was over.

At approximately the same time, two Scotland Yard detectives – DI

Ian Forbes and DS Tom Parry – were arriving at Stafford railway station. Arthur Rees, the Chief Constable of Staffordshire, had been so certain that Christine's body would be found in his county that he had taken the highly unusual decision to call in Scotland Yard before the body was found. At Stafford station, Chief Superintendent Harry Bailey, head of the Staffordshire CID, introduced himself to the two Metropolitan officers. These three men were to form the nucleus of the team dedicated to finding the killer of Christine Darby. Harry Bailey took the Met officers to police HQ in Stafford to meet the Chief Constable, but no sooner had they arrived there than the news came through that a girl's body had been found on Cannock Chase. Formalities were quickly abandoned, and within minutes they were taken down the A34 to the location, arriving just after 6 pm.

In his autobiography, *Squad Man*, Ian Forbes recalls the moment he saw Christine's body. He admits that, as well as anger, he experienced an initial fear that he might not manage to catch Christine's murderer. However, his rage soon turned to cold determination that nothing would ever stop him from tracking down the culprit. Tom Parry was feeling the same emotion. Turning to Ian, he said, 'Good God, guv'nor, that could have been my little girl. We've got to find this bastard.'

Although there had been no formal identification, there was no doubt that this was the body of Christine Darby. Although the trousers and one plimsoll were missing, she was wearing the white T-shirt with a floral pattern, white ankle socks and blue nylon underskirt. The soles of the ankle socks were still clean, indicating that the girl had probably been carried to the spot. While police photographers took pictures of the body, Harry Bailey, Ian Forbes and Tom Parry began a search of the immediate area, which had been sealed off, finding the missing trousers in bracken about 30 yards from the body.

A tent was erected over the scene and floodlights installed. The Home Office pathologist, Dr Alan Usher, was in Sheffield and did not arrive until 11 o'clock to make his initial on-the-spot examination. It was the early hours of Wednesday morning before the body could be taken to Staffordshire Infirmary for Dr Usher's post-mortem. This was carried out immediately, and was completed by 6 am. It proved that the girl had met her death on Saturday afternoon. She had died from suffocation, and bruising on her left cheek indicated that this was either due to pressure of the killer's hand over her mouth and nose, or to her face being pushed into a cushion or pillow. She had been sexually assaulted, and there were indications that this had probably occurred at the place where she was found. Dr Usher thought that she had lost consciousness after 10 or 20 seconds, dying about two minutes later. The sexual assault had probably occurred while she was unconscious. There were no scratches and bruises, apart from the one on her face, which made it likely that she had not been able to put up a struggle.

On Wednesday morning, Ian Forbes and Harry Bailey returned to Plantation 110, to check out the two fire rides. These are avenues which run through the trees, and are designed to check the spread of forest fires. They are wide enough for a car to drive down, though not wide enough for it to turn round; anyone driving down a fire ride would have to reverse to get out again. As they detectives had hoped, they found tyre tracks on one of the rides. The tracks led 140 yards down the ride to a spot close to the murder location. The fact that a car had driven so far into the ride and then reversed the same distance made Ian Forbes revise his initial theory that the murder had happened in the dark. At night, the killer would surely not have driven, then reversed, for 140 yards. It now seemed more likely that the manoeuvre had taken place by daylight.

Photographs of the tracks were taken and sent to Joseph Wilson of the Pirelli Tyre Co for expert analysis. He found that there was insufficient tread to identify the make of tyres, but after measuring the distance between the tracks he concluded that they had probably been made by a Ford Corsair, a Ford Cortina or an Austin A60.

On the three weekends following the murder, police checkpoints were set up on all roads leading to Cannock Chase. Motorists were asked if they had visited the Chase on Saturday 19th August after 2.30 pm. Thousands of handbills were distributed with a picture of Christine Darby on one side and a map showing the murder location on the other.

In the following weeks of the murder inquiry, the police received full public co-operation, often from surprising people. Known criminals, whose doors were normally slammed in the face of any visiting police officer, reacted differently in this situation, pledging their full support for the investigation. Other people came forward too: lovers who had been on Cannock Chase that weekend gave information to the murder squad, trusting the police to keep their secrets. The people of Walsall contributed to a £2,000 reward fund to be paid to anyone who gave information leading to the arrest and conviction of the killer. Much of it was sent by children donating their pocket money. Everyone wanted to help.

Jeanne Rawlings of Wolverhampton reported seeing a grey Austin Cambridge on Cannock Chase at 4.20 pm on the afternoon of the murder. Victor Whitehouse of Hednesford told the police that he was walking his dog along one of the narrow fire rides when he saw a man standing by the open door of a blue-grey car, half hidden by a fallen tree. He thought the car was an Austin A55 or A60. His description of the man, together with Jeanne Rawlings's information, led the police to draw up a profile of a man of 35–40, about 5 ft 10 in tall, with broad shoulders, dark hair and an oval-shaped face. They knew he drove a grey Austin car, and believed he had a Walsall accent.

Despite the reservations that many of the police officers had, it was decided to compile an Identikit profile. The system had been brought to the UK in 1961, and Ian Forbes sent for the country's leading expert, DS John Talbot of Scotland Yard. John Talbot came to Cannock and interviewed Mrs Rawlings and Mr Whitehouse separately, asking them to select, from a range of chins, mouths, hairlines, hairstyles and eyes, those that matched the man they had seen on Cannock Chase. Except for the eyes, each witness chose exactly the same facial features. An Identikit face was drawn, and both witnesses agreed it was like the man they had seen.

Ian Forbes and Harry Bailey decided to circulate the Identikit profile firstly in the official wanted list, the *Police Gazette*. Then, when they were sure that every police officer in the land had seen it, it was released to the national press. In the next two days, 1,000 calls were received from people who were sure they knew someone like the picture. According to Tom Parry, it was bedlam! Hundreds of letters were received too. Most were helpful, though sadly a few were from cranks claiming to be the killer. All had to be carefully checked out, of course.

One letter came from Lewis Williams, a staff artist on the *Birmingham Mail*, pointing out that many people, particularly children, would not be able to relate the flat, black and white Identikit picture to a real living face. He offered to flesh out the picture in colour, giving it facial contours, and the police were very willing to accept his help. Checking continually with Jeanne Rawlings and Victor Whitehouse and making amendments in the light of their comments, Williams was able to paint a face that now had a more lifelike bone structure, more light and shade. Two thousand colour posters were printed and distributed to all police stations, and for the first time a coloured wanted poster was used in the *Police Gazette*.

DO YOU KNOW HIM?

Tell the police

The police want to interview this man in connection with the Christine Darby murder.

Age 35-40, height 5ft. 10in. medium build with broad shoulders, black hair brushed back, reddish complexion

Express & Star

The 'Wanted' poster. (*Express & Star*)

The other lead was, of course, the grey Austin car. The investigating team checked out 1,375,000 vehicle taxation files, and interviewed 80,000 people through the Black Country. In addition, the police tracked down every owner of a grey Austin A55 or A60 who had gone abroad, tracing people to countries as widespread as Australia, Nigeria, Singapore and Canada.

In Walsall, the police had to work shifts to cover the hours from 9 am until midnight, with the majority of officers visiting people in the evenings when more of them would be at home. In the first five weeks of the inquiry, more than 28,000 men between 21 and 50 were interviewed and eliminated from the inquiry. Where any officer had the least doubt about anyone, the man was interviewed at HQ by Ian Forbes or Harry Bailey. Although there were 64 of these interviewees, including 18 self-confessed peeping Toms, none proved to be the wanted man.

Weeks turned into months. In August 1968, after a year working on the case, Ian Forbes took a four-week holiday with his wife, and Tom Parry went on a senior CID course. Rumours began to circulate in Walsall that the two men had given up on the case and gone back to Scotland Yard. This was far from the truth, but Ian Forbes deliberately did nothing to counter these stories.

Then, on 4th November, another Walsall girl was approached. Margaret Aulton, aged ten, was on her own on a piece of waste ground on the corner of Bridgeman Street and Queen Street. She was making some final adjustments to the bonfire she had built earlier with her family. It was 7.45 pm when a man walked up to her and asked if she would like some fireworks. He seemed pleasant enough, and she followed him to his car. He opened the passenger door, telling Margaret, 'They're in there.' The girl could not see any fireworks and backed away, but the man tried to manhandle her into the car. She broke free, and the man suddenly became aware of a young woman watching the encounter from the doorway of the local chip shop. He got in his car and drove off.

The woman who had witnessed the event was 18 year old Wendy Lane, who had the good sense to realise what was going on, and to memorise the car's registration number. The police were called and Wendy reported the incident to them, telling them that the car was a green and white Ford Corsair with the number 429 LOP. However, when the registration was checked, the police drew a blank. The number 429 LOP belonged to a Ford Anglia kept at Castleford in

Yorkshire. It seemed that the inquiry into the incident was over before it had begun, but luckily the three investigating detectives were dogged characters. They decided to check out every vehicle with the registration letters LOP. There were 999 of them, but only 24 were Ford Corsairs, and of these only one was green and white. Its number was 492 LOP and, significantly, it was owned by a Walsall man. He was Raymond Leslie Morris who lived in a flat in Regent House, almost opposite Walsall police station!

The next day, 5th November, two detectives visited Raymond Morris at his place of employment, a precision engineering factory at Oldbury. The detectives told Morris that they wanted to interview him about an incident in Walsall the previous evening. The men drove back to Walsall police station in Raymond Morris's Corsair, and the police officers noted that Morris did not ask why he was being taken in.

In the police station, the officers – now joined by a Staffordshire CID officer – told Morris that they were investigating an incident in which a young girl had been approached by a man offering her fireworks. When they suggested that Morris could be that man, he denied it, saying, 'Who told you this? This is too ridiculous for words.' He told the officers that he had left work at 7 pm and would have been home at about 7.35 pm, ten minutes before the incident occurred. He invited them to check with his wife. Asked if he knew Bridgeman Street, he said that he did, but that he never took that way home, except on Saturday afternoons when he called at a car wash in St Michael's Road. This immediately interested his questioners, since the car wash was close to the Camden Street–Corporation Street junction where Christine Darby had been abducted.

When the officers requested that Raymond Morris should take part in an identity parade, he initially agreed, but then refused, saying that he wanted to phone his solicitor first. He rang John Benton, who had handled his divorce from his first wife, and then, on his advice, agreed to take part in the identity parade. At the parade, Morris became nervous and agitated, but calmed down when both Wendy Lane and Margaret Aulton failed to pick him out.

The police were disappointed with this outcome, but continued to be very suspicious of Morris. They decided to follow him home from work, and found that he regularly passed the location where Christine Darby was kidnapped. Moreover, he pronounced Caldmore Green in the local manner, and, apart from his hairstyle, he matched the Identikit picture of the man sought for Christine Darby's murder. Police also

Raymond Morris. (*Express & Star*)

found that a complaint had been made against him in October 1966, alleging that he had taken two young girls to his flat in Regent House and partially undressed them. Morris had denied the offence, and because there was no corroborative evidence, no charges had been brought.

When the police checked their files, they found that the name of Raymond Leslie Morris cropped up several times earlier. He had been interviewed three times. Records at Cannock police station showed that at the time of the Mansty Gully murder inquiry, a Peter Morris had told the police that his brother Raymond was a man of abnormal sexual feelings, who could have been responsible for murdering the two girls.

Seventeen days after the Christine Darby murder, Raymond Morris had been one of the owners of grey cars questioned. On that occasion, he had said that he had left work at 1 o'clock on the Saturday afternoon, arrived home at 1.45, spent the afternoon shopping in Walsall with his wife, and visited his mother-in-law's home at about 4.30 pm. Morris's young second wife, Carol, had confirmed this version of events. Later, when the grey car was examined, the police officers were surprised, given that the couple had no children, to find a toy panda and a ball. Morris said that the toys belonged to a young child who had stayed with them during August. Again Carol Morris corroborated her husband's statement.

The third time Morris had been interviewed was as part of a massive door-to-door inquiry in February 1968, when the police were checking the alibis of every man between 20 and 50. When questioned, Raymond Morris reacted angrily at first, saying that the police were trying to catch him out, to see if he made any minor changes in his story. Since these officers knew nothing of his earlier interview, they were rather surprised at his reaction to a routine inquiry. However, he stuck to the same story as before, and Carol Morris backed him up, leaving the police officers feeling dissatisfied but unable to shake his alibi.

On 15th November 1968, Ian Forbes and Harry Bailey decided to detain Morris, arresting him at 7.30 am as he was on his way to work. When DCI Pat Molloy told him he was being arrested in connection with the murder of Christine Darby, Morris blurted out, 'Oh God, is it my wife?' This confirmed to Ian Forbes that Carol Morris held the key to proving that her husband was the killer.

At 10.30 that morning, Carol Morris was called out of the wages office where she worked, and told that her husband had been arrested. Carol's world fell apart. She was 25, 14 years younger than Raymond, and she was devoted to him. She agreed to return with the police officers to the flat in Regent House, where clothing and other items belonging to her husband were collected for scientific examination. That afternoon, she was interviewed at Hednesford police station by Ian Forbes and Harry Bailey. After a great deal of thought and reflection, Carol said for the first time that she might have been wrong when she had said that Raymond Morris had returned home at about 2 o'clock on the afternoon of the murder. She said that she had not been lying but that she had trusted her husband completely and had made 'an honest mistake'. She now said that she could not possibly be sure of anything about that afternoon.

With the suspect's alibi gone, Forbes and Bailey travelled to Stafford police station where Raymond Morris was being held. Together with Tom Parry and Pat Molloy, they interviewed Morris. Although he seemed frightened, he maintained a defiant attitude, denying his guilt and sticking to his original account of how he had spent the Saturday afternoon. Five times he was asked to take part in an identity parade, and each time he refused absolutely. However, the next morning, Pat Molloy brought Victor Whitehouse to the station and in the station yard he identified Morris as the man he had seen on Cannock Chase on the afternoon of the murder.

Ten days later, Carol Morris made a new statement, saying that her husband had come home at 4.30 pm that afternoon. It was then that they had gone out to buy some cakes for her mother. Mrs Edith Pearse made a statement that when her daughter and son-in-law had arrived at her home, Raymond had apologised, saying they were late because he had had to stay on at work. However, his works time card proved that he had clocked off at 1.13 pm that day. Between that time and 4.30 pm he had no alibi at all.

Carol made this new statement after being shown a number of pornographic photographs found in a box in the spare bedroom of the Regent House flat. All involved female children. Some of them had been taken by means of a delayed-action shutter, and showed Carol's five year old cousin being indecently touched by her husband. Although his face was not on the photographs, the hand on the picture was wearing Raymond's silver wrist watch. For the police, this explained a peculiar event that happened at Winson Green prison, where Morris was taken after his arrest. When the reception officer searched him, he was found to be wearing his distinctive wrist watch strapped around his ankle, under his sock!

Ian Forbes admits being concerned that he might be accused by defence lawyers of bullying the distraught wife of the accused man into changing her alibi statement. He was therefore touched and relieved to receive a Christmas card at Cannock police station, signed 'With best wishes from Carol Morris'. If needed, this was tangible evidence that Carol, far from feeling intimidated, held him in high regard.

At his trial before Mr Justice Ashworth in February 1969, Raymond Leslie Morris was accused of four charges: the murder of Christine Darby on 19th August 1967; the attempted abduction of Margaret Aulton on 4th November 1968; indecent assault on the child in the photographs in 1967; and indecent assault on the same child in 1968.

Before the trial began, Kenneth Mynett QC, the defence counsel, put forward a strong application for three separate trials for the charges, on the grounds that it would be impossible for the jury to give Morris a fair trial on the murder charge if evidence was put before them relating to the other charges. Mr Mynett also suggested that there was no evidence put forward relating to the third charge, which should therefore be quashed.

On the last point Mr Justice Ashworth agreed, and that charge was allowed to 'lie on the file'. On the matter of hearing the remaining three offences in one trial, he said that the introduction of evidence on the attempted abduction and the indecent assault *would* gravely prejudice the accused man's interest. However, it was equally important that justice should be done, and accordingly he was ruling that all three charges should be tried together. This was a vital decision for the prosecution. All of the evidence against Raymond Morris was circumstantial. Taken together, it added up to an extremely strong case; divided into three, it would have been much weaker.

Morris was now charged with the murder of Christine Darby, the attempted abduction of Margaret Aulton, and the indecent assault against the girl in the photographs. He pleaded not guilty to the murder and attempted assault, but guilty to the indecent assault. This was the first time he had admitted any offence at all; little wonder, then, that his defence counsel had wanted it dealt with in a separate hearing.

The prosecution, led by Brian Gibbens QC, marshalled the evidence against the accused man: two witnesses who had seen him near the spot where Christine Darby's body was found; the grey car used in the murder case being like the one Morris owned; the false alibis Morris had given in both cases; his constant refusal to take part in an identity parade. Gibbens drew parallels between the lies used to entice Christine Darby into the grey car, and the lies told to Margaret Aulton to get her to walk over to the green and white Corsair. He pointed out that the photographic evidence of Morris committing an offence against a girl – an offence now admitted – revealed a similar type of activity to the assault on Christine Darby. Mr Gibbens referred to the wrist watch found strapped to Morris's ankle after his first court appearance on the

The car used by Raymond Morris to abduct Christine Darby was bought by a Black Country garage owner, who destroyed it by fire. (*Express & Star*)

murder charge, and commented that it was only after the discovery of the photographs that its significance was realised.

The circumstantial evidence against Raymond Morris amounted to a formidable case, and the witnesses impressed the jury. At the end of the seven-day trial, the judge warned the jury against thinking that if Morris had committed one offence, he must have committed the others. After summing up the evidence, he advised the jury: 'Justice includes two things – acquitting the innocent or those you have any doubts about, but Justice also includes convicting the guilty when we are sure. If your consciences are right, your verdicts will be right.'

The jury – nine men and three women – retired for less than two hours before returning a verdict of guilty to both the murder and the attempted abduction. Mr Justice Ashworth sentenced Raymond Morris to life imprisonment for the murder of Christine Darby, three years' imprisonment for the attempted abduction of Margaret Aulton, and one year for the indecent assault.

The judge then added: 'There must be many mothers in Walsall and the area whose hearts will beat more lightly as a result of this verdict.' To Ian Forbes he said: 'It must be a great satisfaction to you to know that all your efforts have been rewarded by what, for my part, I believe to be the right result. The people of this county and of the whole country owe a debt of gratitude to you and those who served under you for what you have done.'

After the case, Ian Forbes summed up Raymond Morris as 'the most evil and sadistic man I ever had the ill luck to encounter'.

14

THE
SOLDIER'S NIGHTMARE

The Murder of Judith Roberts at Wigginton, near Tamworth
June 1972

Judith Roberts went missing from her home in Tamworth at 6 pm on Wednesday 7th June 1972. She had had a minor tiff with her parents because she did not want to eat all her tea. Like many 14 year old girls, she thought that her legs were not slim enough and that she needed to diet. Like most parents of teenagers, Vince and Julia Roberts were keen that their daughter should eat a proper, balanced meal. Feeling hard done by, Judith went upstairs to do her homework with her twin sister, but then decided that she would get out her bike and go for a ride. At 6.30 pm, a teacher from her school saw Judith riding her bike towards Wigginton. But then every parent's worst nightmare scenario began: Judith never returned from her ride and her anxious parents had to ring the police.

A massive police search was put into effect that night, and continued for the next three days. A description of the girl was circulated: Judith was 5 ft 1 in, with fair hair and blue eyes, and had a brace on her top front teeth. She was wearing her school uniform: a blue and white check dress, a navy blue anorak and black lace-up shoes. She was riding a green Raleigh bicycle.

Tracker dogs were used, and officers from Lichfield, Burton upon Trent, Brownhills and Aldridge were brought in. Two hundred police personnel were involved in the search, together with a large number of volunteers, including soldiers from the nearby Whittington barracks. The search ended at 4.30 pm on Saturday 10th June, when Junior Private Barry Gibson spotted Judith's green bike lying in a potato field off Comberford Road, Wigginton. Sixteen year old Barry, from Wolverhampton, recalled: 'We saw this field with very high hedges. I

The murder scene. (John Walker)

walked in and stood waiting for four other people. Then I saw the bicycle.' He was soon joined by his fellow soldiers, and it was Junior Lance Corporal Trevor Steele who spotted an anorak. He had found the body of the missing girl, lying partially hidden under sacks and corrugated sheeting. She had been battered to death.

The spot – a field surrounded by 12-foot high hawthorn hedges – was about a mile from Judith's home. Police immediately sealed off the area, erecting a white plastic tent over Judith's body. Next to Judith's body were a metal pole and a jagged piece of asbestos. Forensic investigations soon proved that it was the piece of asbestos that had been used to kill the young schoolgirl. Although the lower half of Judith's body was naked, she had not been sexually violated.

Quickly on the scene were the Chief Constable, Arthur Rees, Assistant Chief Constable (crime) Harry Bailey, and the head of Staffordshire CID, Detective Chief Superintendent Harold Wright. It was not long before the decision was made to call in Scotland Yard, and Detective Chief Superintendent Donald Saunders arrived to take charge of the murder hunt. Don Saunders thought that someone might be shielding the killer, and urged anyone with information to come forward. He said that photographs of the area, taken from an RAF helicopter, were proving useful, and asked the owner of a dark red saloon car, seen near the murder spot on the evening of 7th June, to

A tent was erected over the spot where Judith's body was found. Conferring are Detective Superintendent Frank Jordan, Assistant Chief Constable Harry Bailey and Detective Chief Superintendent Harold Wright. (*Express & Star*)

contact the police. He also wished to trace the drivers of a white Triumph 2000 and a yellow articulated tanker seen in the area. He appealed for 'shy' courting couples who had used the Comberford Lane area during the spring and summer to come forward, promising them that their information would be treated in confidence.

Of particular interest to the police was a tall, 'husky', thickset man who tried to lure a young girl into his car in Whittington on 7th June. Shortly after the murder of Judith Roberts, the alarm was raised when a 15 year old girl disappeared from her Tamworth home, but on this occasion the missing girl was found at her boyfriend's home in Barton-under-Needwood.

A murder incident room was set up in Tamworth at St Editha's church hall, to act as the nerve centre of the operation, and police officers began the mammoth task of asking all men in the north Tamworth/ Wigginton area to allow their fingerprints to be taken and sent to the Midlands criminal record office for examination. This fingerprinting later widened to take in the villages of Comberford, Harlaston, Elford, Newton Regis, No Man's Heath, Botany Bay and even parts of Lichfield.

The police appeal for witnesses. (*Express & Star*)

A week after the murder, Judith's twin sister Ann courageously agreed, despite her own grief at the loss of her sister, to take part in a re-enactment of the murdered girl's last cycle ride, hoping to jog the memories of anyone who might have witnessed something.

Saturday 24th June was carnival day in Tamworth, but in 1972 the festivities were less joyful than usual, as it was also the day of Judith Roberts' funeral. Three hundred people stood outside St Editha's church as the funeral procession arrived. Market traders stopped doing business as the coffin was taken into church. In his address, the vicar of Tamworth, the Rev Albert Edwards, expressed the sympathy of the whole town to Judith's parents, her twin sister Ann and her younger sisters, saying, 'This is a very dark time for them and for our community.' The funeral was also attended by Detective Chief Superintendents Donald Saunders and Harold Wright.

After the funeral, the police said that they wished to talk to a man and woman with a pushchair who had watched Judith's funeral, together with a soldier in uniform seen with them. All three of these people were traced and eliminated from the inquiry. At this stage of the inquiry, the police revealed that they wished to trace a schoolgirl and a tall, well-built man seen talking at the entrance to Comberford Lane, Wigginton, between 6.30 pm and 7.30 pm on 7th June. The girl had been pushing a cycle similar to Judith's, and the man had been carrying something.

The various lines of inquiry seemed to be leading nowhere until a bespectacled young man, living with his grandmother in Longton, Stoke-on-Trent, had a series of dreams in which he saw the face of a murdered girl. Andrew Evans had been a boy soldier at Whittington barracks, about four miles from Tamworth, at the time of Judith Roberts' death. On the day before the murder, he had been informed that his asthma made him unfit to stay in the army. He had gone to live with his grandmother in Longton and found a job as a salesman. Worried by his dreams, Andrew went into his local police station on 9th October and asked to see a picture of Judith Roberts. He did not come out again. He was interviewed first in Longton, then taken to Tamworth for further questioning. Two days later, he was charged with Judith Roberts' murder.

When Andrew appeared in court in April 1973, the prosecution counsel, Mr Brian Gibbens QC, stated that in 'a number of remarkable interviews' Evans kept asking to see a picture of Judith to see if the girl in his dream was the girl who had been killed. The prosecution alleged that, during these interviews, Andrew Evans had admitted to the police that he had killed Judith Roberts, saying, 'I know I did it. Do you think I did it?' According to the prosecution, many of the details revealed by Evans could only have been known to the killer, because certain facts had not been publicised.

Mr Gibbens said that in one of his statements, Evans had stated, 'it was in the afternoon and I walked out of the barracks by the back way. I was in my uniform. I had nothing to do that day, and I went for a think – thinking about what was going to happen when they chucked me out.' Evans said that he had stood in a field, with his arms behind his back. His statement continued, 'Then I saw the girl cycling along and I called for help. She stopped cycling and I pulled her off her cycle. I then hit her in the face with my fist. We did not struggle. I dragged her across a field. She was limp. Then I laid her down. She had bruises on her face. She started to come round and tried to push me away. I hit her on the side of her face and she fell back. I dragged her by the arms and legs to the hedge. I hit her with something. I don't remember any more until I got back to the barracks. Something must have made me very, very angry for me to hit this girl.'

Mr Gibbens told the jury of six men and six women that a great deal depended on the young man's confession, which had been made over three days to a police officer. He had no doubt that the jury would have a great deal of sympathy for the defendant because it was a sad case, but he reminded them that they would have to decide whether he was the one who had committed the murder.

The jury was shown a piece of bloodstained corrugated asbestos, and pathologist Dr Van de Merwe gave evidence that it was probably the murder weapon. In answer to questions from Mr John Owen QC, the defence counsel, the pathologist agreed that the absence of asbestos particles in the hair or head wounds of the dead girl raised some doubts about this. However, he was sure that the piece of asbestos was consistent with the injuries, and believed that it was likely to have been the murder weapon. A length of metal post had been found by the body, but was ruled out as it had no signs of blood on it.

DS Roy Williamson said that Andrew Evans had told him, 'I can see a picture of it. I can see her lying near a hedge with her brown hair and parka over her face.' Asked if he had a mental picture of the murderer, Evans was alleged to have said, 'He is a small youth, about 5 ft 4 in, with dark hair.' When the police first interviewed Evans, he asked them what would happen to someone who had committed the murder. DS Williamson said that he had replied, 'He would be in some considerable trouble, apart from wanting his head looking into by a psychiatrist.' DS Rex Dinsdale, who saw Evans later in the incident room at Tamworth, gave evidence that the defendant was shaking and had started to cry.

Private Ron Pearson gave evidence that Evans had become very upset when he learned that he was to be discharged because of asthma. Private Peter Ogden, who shared a barrack room with Evans, said that on 7th June 1972, the defendant was left to do light duties while the other trainees took part in physical training. Evans was not there when they returned, and did not turn up until 10 pm. Questioned by the defence about an earlier differing statement, Ogden admitted that he could not really remember what happened that day.

DS Terence Reader gave evidence that when Mrs Evans had come to see her son at Tamworth police station, Andrew had said to her, 'It's no good, mum. I have done it. I have told them all about it.'

Mrs Evans told the court that Andrew had suffered from asthma from the age of four. He always wanted to do what other children did, but she had told him it was not possible. She said that Andrew had never been violent in any way, and used to 'get the worst end of it' at school because he could not fight back.

The Scotland Yard detective in charge of the murder hunt, Chief Superintendent Don Saunders, answered questions about a Mr X, an early suspect in the inquiry and a man alleged by the defence to possess a violent attitude to women. Don Saunders said that the police inquiries into this man had been in very great depth. He agreed that the man had at first denied being at the place of Judith's murder, then later admitted it. He also agreed that blood found on the man's coat was of the same group as Judith's. However, the blood group was shared by 45 per cent of the population, including Mr X himself. The police had uncovered no evidence at all that Mr X had anything to do with the murder.

Questioned by his defence counsel, Andrew Evans said that he had a 'recollection' of leaning against a gate and looking into a field. On the other side of the field was a man standing up, and right next to him was a girl's leg sticking up. He had also dreamed of seeing a girl's face that he could not place. The next day he had gone to the police station, to see if this face was the face of the murdered girl. He agreed with his counsel that he had seen a photograph of the murdered girl before drugs had been administered to him, at his own request, to help his memory. He stated that after being interviewed by two police officers, he went to bed worried, because he was not sure of anything.

Cross-examined by the prosecution, Andrew admitted that he had told police officers more than once that he had killed the girl, adding, 'I thought I was telling the truth but I now know that I wasn't.'

When his defence counsel asked him whether anything he had heard in court suggested that he might have killed the girl, Andrew Evans replied, 'No, quite the contrary. I know now I didn't do it.' Asked what he could remember of his movements on 7th June, Andrew insisted that he had not left Whittington barracks that day. Asked what he had read or seen about the murder of Judith Roberts, the defendant said that he had watched a television programme of the reconstruction of the girl's last cycle ride, with the girl's twin sister taking her role.

Opening the defence case, John Owen pointed out that the only evidence against Andrew Evans was what he had told the police. He had told them – and, indeed, had written down – that he had killed the girl, but what the jury should bear in mind was that throughout he had been talking from a memory which everyone agreed was not a full memory. 'You may think,' John Owen continued, 'that he must have convinced himself that he had committed the crime.' One possible explanation for the youth's partial recollection of seeing the girl might be that he had in fact witnessed the killing and been shocked by what he saw. Evans had undergone tests with drugs in an attempt to jog his memory, and was now satisfied that he had not committed the murder.

Psychiatrist Dr John Stephens described Andrew Evans as a minor version of Walter Mitty, in that he had a very great ability to create fantasies of his own in compensation for certain problems. He subsequently could not distinguish between the fantasy and the bedrock of fact which might have been there to start with. Asked by the judge, Mr Justice Crichton, whether Evans could have imagined killing the girl if he had no personal involvement in the crime, Dr Stephens replied that it was just possible, but that Evans was more likely to have imagined committing the murder if he had witnessed someone else killing the girl and had not gone to her aid.

Asked by the defence whether Evans's statements of confession had any validity, Dr Stephens stated, 'From my knowledge of him, very little validity indeed.' The doctor told the jury that the defendant had asked for drugs to jog his memory, and in one session had recalled being in a field and seeing a girl and a man struggling. Dr Stephens described Evans as immature, ineffective and inoffensive, adding, 'I have seen him on occasions desperate to convince himself he hasn't done this, and on other occasions just as desperate to convince himself that he has. I think that he does not know the answer to whether he did or did not do it.'

Prison medical officer Dr Reginald Washbrook said that he had examined Evans on numerous occasions and found him to be an inadequate person with an element of drama within his make-up. He considered that when Evans made statements to the police, he was telling the truth that existed in his mind. It was a possibility that Evans had been at the barracks all day; it was also a possibility that he was in the field, murdering the girl.

In his summing-up for the prosecution, Brian Gibbens pointed out to the jury that Andrew Evans had over a period of three and a half days made repeated confessions of his guilt. Everyone in court was very saddened not only by the death of the girl, but by the fate of the young man. He had joined the army, tried too hard, and brought on an attack of asthma. He was discharged from the army and might have been in a turbulent state of mind. Mr Gibbens said that the man referred to as Mr X had been thoroughly investigated by the police and had adamantly denied the offence. The defence suggestion that he was the real murderer was a blatant red herring.

In his closing speech for the defence, John Owen said that Andrew Evans could have become 'punch drunk' because of the number of people who had interrogated him. Everybody had been having a go at Evans to see what they could find. One thing was clear: the defendant did not know anything now, and could not rely on anything that came into his mind. Counsel said that he believed Evans's personality was such that he could convince himself that he had committed an offence when he had not.

After the judge's summing-up, the jury retired to consider their verdict. When they returned, it was to find Andrew Evans guilty of murdering Judith Roberts. The judge sentenced him to be detained for life, but in a 30-second reappearance in court on 17th April, the judge said that he had made an error in his wording. Evans was sentenced to be detained during Her Majesty's pleasure. 'It really amounts to the same thing,' Mr Justice Crichton commented.

Evans was advised that he had no grounds for appeal. He was also told by his fellow-inmates in prison that continuing to protest his innocence meant that he would stand no chance of ever being released. He took their advice, became a 'model prisoner', and by 1988 had been moved to an open prison at Leyhill, Gloucestershire. He was allowed several privileges, including home leave, attending college courses, and working at the Slimbridge wildlife reserve. However, in 1991, when a local Tamworth researcher concluded that he could not be guilty, Evans approached the prison governor and stated that he was no longer prepared to admit his guilt. As he expected, he was immediately transferred to a high security prison at the Verne, Weymouth. He is still there, and still protests his innocence. His case is supported by the legal reform group Justice, and was twice featured on the *Crime Stalker* television programme in 1995. In the second of these programmes, two of Evans's former classmates – Susie Gower and Maureen Agrelo – came forward to say that, as a boy, Andrew would frequently try to gain peer acceptance by taking the blame for things he had not done. John Stalker questioned his conviction on confession-only evidence, painting him as a 'Billy Liar' character.

On the other hand, I spoke recently to a former police officer who was involved with questioning Andrew at Tamworth police station. He told me, 'Andrew Evans was rather pathetic, really. I am convinced that he had come in to confess. He was suffering from feelings of guilt and needed to get it off his chest.'

BIBLIOGRAPHY

Andrews, Allen *Intensive Inquiries* (1973)

Bentley, Ian *A History of the Staffordshire Police Force*

Brashay, Fred and Grant, Wendy *Going Back* (1992)

Farran, Roy *Winged Dagger: Adventures on Special Service* (1948, republished 1986)

Forbes, Ian *Squad Man* (1973)

Gaute, J H H & Odell, R *The New Murderers' Who's Who* (1989)

Godwin, John *The Murder of Christina Collins* (1990)

Godwin, John *The Pocket Palmer* (1992)

Hawkes, Harry *Murder on the A34* (1970)

Hoskins, Percy *The Sound of Murder* (1973)

Lane, Brian (ed.) *The Murder Club Guide to The Midlands* (1988)

Lloyd, Georgina *Murders Unspeakable* (1993)

Lucas, Norman *The Child Killers* (1970)

Millen, Ernest *Specialist In Crime* (1972)

Posner, Michael *Midlands Murders* (1973)

Prince, Rosalind *Capital Crimes* (1994)

Prince, Rosalind *Some Staffordshire Murders* (1983)

Tullet, Tom *Murder Squad* (1981)

Wilson, Colin and Pitman, Patricia *Encyclopedia of Murder* (1984)

Wilson, Colin and Seaman, Donald *Encyclopedia of Modern Murder* (1989)

INDEX

INDEX